THE WAITING
TRUE SELF

Guidance for Discovery
with the I CHING

MC FLENNIKEN

ISBN: 979-8-9890533-0-8 (Paperback)
979-8–9890533-1-5 (ebook)
Library of Congress Control Number: 2023917266
Publisher's Cataloging-in-Publication data

Names: Flenniken, M. C., author.
Title: The Waiting True Self: Guidance for Discovery with the I Ching / M. C. Flenniken.
Description: Includes bibliographical references. | Tucson, AZ: MC Flenniken, 2023.
Identifiers: LCCN: 2023917266 | ISBN: 979-8-9890533-0-8 (paperback)
Subjects: LCSH: Yi jing. | Self-actualization (Psychology)--Religious aspects--Taoism. | Self help. | BISAC: BODY, MIND & SPIRIT/ I Ching | SELF-HELP / Personal Growth / General | PHILOSOPHY / Taoist
Classification: LCC BL624 .F54 2023 | DDC 158--dc23

Cover Photograph & Design by MC Flenniken © 2023
Cover Image, Lago de Chapala, México
Typesetting & Interior Design by Three Knolls Publishing

To the true self in all of us

Contents

INTRODUCTION

Purportedly one of the oldest books in recorded human history, the written form of the *I Ching*[1] originated in China as a classic of divination more than 3,000 years ago. The *I Ching* is often touted as a book of wisdom (including its many iterations over the centuries), citing historical figures such as Lao-tse and Confucius who utilized it in the formation of their philosophies.[2] From my nearly four decades of working almost daily with the *I Ching*, I believe it is a distortion to regard the text itself as containing any inherent wisdom.

However, if we switch our focus from the contents of the book to the intelligent Consciousness that is willing to communicate through it, then it can become a true gift. This communication is not "channeling" or any form of mediumship. Rather, it is a process of learning to tap into our innate capacity to relate with and learn from this source.

In referring to this source, I use the term "Cosmic Consciousness" (and sometimes the "Tao within") because these are sufficiently vague terms that avoid the imposition of preconceived ideas which only create obstacles in learning to develop our own relationship with it. Some claim that the "Tao is unknowable" and "cannot be named" — descriptors that give the impression that the "Tao" is also "unrelatable" — which we can discover for ourselves is not the case.

Conceivably millions of people over the centuries have relied on various interpretations of the *I Ching* for guidance in life. But regardless of whatever version of interpretation is used, reliance

---

[1] *In this book, I use the version by Richard Wilhelm and Cary F. Baynes, The I Ching or Book of Changes (Princeton, New Jersey: Bollingen Series XIX, Princeton University Press, 1967).*
[2] *ibid, liv*

on the *I Ching* text alone, without the relational guidance from the Cosmic Consciousness, can never serve as a source for the transformational wisdom, healing and protection that is available. It can only become so through the process of developing a one-on-one exchange with the CC as a teacher that actively relates with the human consciousness of the learner.

The *I Ching* therefore can be thought of as a dialog between the Cosmic Consciousness (CC) and human beings, if it is used effectively. Using it effectively means learning how to allow the CC to lead us in the interpretation of the metaphors intended as guidance from within the text, which is the focus of this book. As will be described in upcoming Chapters, this dialog is a form of "education" available to us. By applying what we learn, it is possible to create movement toward optimum physical and mental health, more harmonious relationships, protection for ourself and others and, ultimately, movement toward expressing our full potential.

If a person is willing to explore receiving guidance from within a teacher-student mode, it is possible to learn how to navigate through the metaphorical language of the *I Ching*. This means identifying the dynamic meanings of a word, phrase, or image that the CC has underscored as guidance. These have meanings that are specific and unique to each individual situation. It is guidance that is responding to the state of our psyche in the moment. Fundamentally it is the energetic exchange between the CC and our consciousness, which will be discussed further in Chapters Two and Four. Over time, we learn to gain trust in this exchange process by continuing to ask questions and clarifying the answers, until the light of penetration subtly emerges. This does not require a special talent or mystical wisdom: it takes perseverance. In ancient times, the *I Ching* was designated for priests and magicians — who very likely misunderstood its true purpose, particularly if the text was being regarded as the exclusive domain for a certain group of people. But through the evolution of human consciousness, we can learn to relate with the CC in personal, authentic and harmonious ways. Then we become conscious participants in our own transformations.

When beginning this journey, we often face uncertainty and doubt. At this point, we might receive this line from Hexagram 4, Youthful Folly: "*When the spring gushes forth, it does not know at first where it will go. But its steady flow fills up the deep place blocking its progress, and success is attained.*" What does "success" mean? If we allow it, the CC helps us to discover how success applies to a given situation: how to harvest gain from any event; how to avoid misfortune as well as how to reinterpret misfortune if it has occurred; how to use our innate abilities to create harmonious living environments; how to heal our bodies; how to relate to the CC in effective ways. Success also means learning to dismantle any self-built dams blocking our life energies. We might present a question through the *I Ching*: "How am I supposed to get out of this situation?" Simply by engaging in the question, one small pebble has been loosened from the dam.

Yet it is so easy to become deflated by listening to the voices of doubt and hesitation or to the voices of other people telling us what to do and what we should fear. When we give validity to falsehoods, it causes us to choose the seemingly safer path of expected behaviors or conventional wisdom. Only to find out later that these solutions led to greater problems. And then we may follow the commonly held practice of blaming ourselves for not listening to our own inner wisdom.

From my years of working with the *I Ching*, I have learned that we are not meant to suffer in the process of living. "*The seed of the good remains, and it is just when the fruit falls to the ground that good sprouts anew from its seed*" (Hexagram 23, Splitting Apart). Regardless of the severity of any trauma or devastating misfortune experienced, "the seed of the good remains." This means our deepest, most fundamental nature is still present, ready to be recognized and to be called upon. In Chapter Five, I discuss some experiences in learning how to facilitate healing from the CC for myself and others following traumatic events.

Utilizing the modality of the *I Ching* offers the potential to develop the singularly most fundamental liaison of our lives: an active kinship with the Consciousness that communicates, teaches and furthers us in all aspects. I believe this Consciousness interacts with us in our lifelong learning process, regardless of whether or not we choose to work with the *I Ching*. As Jung remarked regarding people's acceptance of the *I Ching*, "He who is not pleased by it does not have to use it, and he who is against it is not obliged to find it true. Let it go forth into the world for the benefit of those who can discern its meaning."[3] If we choose to engage in a process of learning from the CC through working with the *I Ching*, we allow it to teach us how to recognize when the false voice of fear, doubt or misperception makes an appearance and to understand where it originated from. It helps us to realize why it's false and the effects it has on us and others. And most importantly, it is the CC that is the source which ultimately dissolves false beliefs and their destructive effects, once we have recognized them. Through this process, we can learn how to remove any obstacles that had been blocking our true nature, allowing it to help lead us through life.

Those who are experienced users of the *I Ching*, as well as those who have never heard of it, may find *"The Waiting True Self"* useful because its ultimate focus is on the development of greater inner freedom, self-acceptance and more harmonious living environments. It is intended as a profound yet practical guide to achieve these ends by learning how to 1) approach a relationship with the CC through the *I Ching*, recognize some of the challenges that may obstruct this relationship and how to overcome them, 2) distinguish

---

[3] *ibid, xxxix*

between our true nature and the constructed or acquired aspects of ourselves, and 3) effectively use our consciousness to create transformations in ourself and our environment.

Perhaps at some point in our lives, we might be moved to reflect: Where does my true nature reside? Why do I feel lost, instead of connected? How do I make the most of my life? Why am I alive? Asking these questions is preparing the ground for growth, prompting us to proceed on our journey. These are promptings from our true self waiting to be discovered, recognized and embraced.

CHAPTER ONE

THE COSMIC CONSCIOUSNESS & THE I CHING

The *I Ching* is an ancient text of metaphors, developed over centuries. It has been studied and interpreted in countless ways. It is a "man-made object" that has quite literally been objectified and studied throughout time by sinologists, mathematicians, philosophers, ancient priests and contemporary teachers. It has endured numerous language translations. The historical text became popularized among English-speaking Western readers in part from the interest expressed by the psychoanalyst, Carl Jung, who utilized the *I Ching* for much of his life, and who wrote the forward for the Princeton University Press edition from which I refer to in brief quotes in this book.

The subtitle to the *I Ching* is *Book of Changes*. In my experience, the metaphor of *"Changes"* refers to each person's life path, not as an arbitrarily changeable process beyond our control, but as the dynamic processes of experience, growth, and evolution of consciousness. The human penchant for the veneration of antiquity and the illusory ease of reliance on external sources for guidance in life, whether that be people or institutions, contribute to the *I Ching* text being misused and misunderstood.

From my 37 years of working with the *I Ching*, I have come to regard it as a great gift, while at the same time, realizing that it contains no inherent wisdom, in and of itself. That is, it cannot be read in order to glean wisdom. In fact, the text is filled with references to many antiquated and patriarchal ideas, yet this need not deter from its gift-nature nor its utility. Similarly, any linguistic or cultural discrepancies and distortions from the original text that might exist also have no bearing on its utility in its present form. **This is because its usefulness lies not in the text itself, but in how the Cosmic Consciousness (CC) dynamically applies the text within the context of each specific situation, in relation to the consciousness of the individual user.**

This book, therefore, is an expression of my working relationship with the CC for almost half my lifetime, using the modality of the *I Ching*. While it is a personal account unique to my life experiences, I believe it reflects universal struggles of existence common to human beings. The fundamental key is the relationship between a receptive learner and the CC that is utilizing the *I Ching* as a method for communication. The potential to develop an active partnership with the CC is as awe-inspiring as it is natural, much like the miraculous nature of our functioning body that we have come to accept as an ordinary fact of life. Over time, we realize that it is the relationship, not the text, that is most essential. Therefore the second half of this book title, "*Guidance for Discovery*," pertains to the development of the two most important relationships in our lives: the relationship with our true self, discussed in Chapter Two, and a working relationship with the Cosmic Consciousness (CC), discussed in Chapters Four and Five.

The discoveries that await are unique, ongoing and emergent within the context of each person's life. I am not referring to "discovering truth," or to finding axioms common to any philosophical or religious tradition. While the *I Ching* mentions "inner truth," this refers to something that is fluid and hidden, yet discoverable. This important concept will be discussed further in this Chapter.

The guidance the CC offers as part of this journey is centered on learning what is harmonious — within ourselves and within any given situation — from a Cosmic Perspective. (I capitalize that term to denote a way of viewing life that is out of the ordinary, and not generally taught or promoted by most societies.) For the purposes of learning from the CC, I utilize only "Book I: The Text," in the *I Ching* which contains the 64 Hexagrams of guidance. I find that the remaining sections, "Book II: The Material" and "Book III: The Commentaries," are not relevant to this purpose.

Ultimately, the focus of our education with the CC involves our journey toward a conscious or active relationship with the CC. As will be discussed in Chapter Two, it is within our innate capacity to form a conscious connection with the CC. This is how we are able to "achieve something great," a phrase that is often mentioned throughout the *I Ching*. This achievement is also referred to as "crossing the water," which means actively relating with the CC. Yet there are times when we accept falsehoods about ourselves and the nature of life. We might doubt our innate capacity to relate with the CC: "It's impossible, sacrilegious, delusional, dangerous." In this situation, *"the great man goes unrecognized,"* as described in Hexagram 1, The Creative. These are times in life when the water becomes dammed and its flow blocked, or when conditions cause the water to evaporate, thus losing our connection with the source of nourishment.

Water Metaphor

Learning to discern guidance from the Cosmic Consciousness involves using our intuition and intellect, as well as perseverance. A significant part of this learning involves overcoming inner prohibitions and disbelief about our ability to actively relate with the CC. Exploring the metaphor of "water" can be useful in illustrating our innate capacity for this relationship.

The element of water is an important metaphor in the *I Ching* to denote the Cosmic Consciousness as well as human consciousness. *"Water flows to unite with water because all parts are subject to the same laws"* (Hexagram 8, Holding Together). Rivers naturally flow to unite with their source, the ocean. The path of the river meanders greatly as it moves along its journey of eventual return to the vast body of water. From the perspective of the *I Ching*, this vast body of water represents the Cosmic Consciousness. This Consciousness flows within all living things, as natural law. The presence of the CC within human beings is what the text refers to as our "true self." During dreams, the CC may appear as some form of water; as rain, a shoreline, ocean waves or even a tsunami that produces no destruction.

Just as a river flows to unite with its source, our true nature unites us with the Cosmic Consciousness. Throughout every journey we make in a lifetime, our "water" nature — our true self — allows us to remain connected with the source of life. Whether we are consciously aware of it or not, the energy of the CC is present in all humans, without exception. It is the subtle voice of the true self that guides us to make a timely decision, to find the right words at the right time and alerts us to a danger. It is the true self that moves us to inspiration, allowing us to create music and art or to recognize the exquisite intelligence in the world of Nature. It is the hint of a soft echo that moves us to seek our true home. If we allow it, the *I Ching* can be a way for us to connect with our true self. Our "water" nature naturally flows toward its source, which means we are innately capable of connecting with it.

The CC does not force itself upon us, but waits for our approach. It is fundamentally our choice or decision whether we engage in the learning process that helps us to embrace our true self. But the ocean in its vast strength has no need to worry about when the river will arrive. Bodies of water might meander around boulders or through mountains that hinder the path, but eventually flow onward toward the goal of returning to the ocean. Hexagram 1, The Creative, assures us that "*confident in his strength, he bides his time....hence ... the time will fulfill itself.*" There is no mandate, obligation, rule, commandment or expectation. The river will eventually flow back to its source, uniting with its origins. We are capable of experiencing this unity in a conscious, intentional way during our life in a body. Regardless of whether or not we make a conscious effort to connect with our true self, we all will eventually experience this unity when we are reunited with the Cosmic Consciousness after we leave life in bodily form.

But it is through intentionally embracing this unity while living in bodily form that allows our consciousness to evolve. This evolution is a growth process that we can actively cultivate and nurture. As mentioned earlier, our active involvement in the process of our evolutionary growth — or unification with our source — is expressed in the text as "crossing the great water." We receive help in this crossing through developing a conscious relationship with the CC (Hexagram 42, Increase): "*If great help comes to a man from on high, this increased strength must be used to achieve something great for which he might otherwise never have found energy, or readiness to take responsibility.*" Further discussion of how the water metaphor may be used is presented later in this Chapter.

Descriptors for the Cosmic Consciousness

If there is a "Cosmic Consciousness" that actively communicates with us utilizing the *I Ching*, what does it have to say about its own nature, drawing from the metaphors contained in the text? What does it say about human nature and our relationship with the CC? Some of the answers to these questions naturally emerged during explorations of specific issues and situations that I have faced over the years, and not from abstract inquiries motivated simply by a desire for information. Below are some metaphors (brief quotes from the *I Ching*) that the CC has indicated as connotations for its own nature:

- the union of movement and strength
- in relation to the universe ... expresses the strong, creative action. In relation to the human world, it denotes the creative

action of the ... sage ... or leader of men, who through his power awakens and develops their higher nature ["leader" refers to both the CC as a whole, and the presence of the CC within each person; it does not endorse the idea of a "higher" or "lower" nature in humans]

- the generating power of the Creative, all beings owe their beginning to it
- energy renewing itself
- inner worth mounts with great force and comes to power
- movement in accord with heaven, producing great power [heaven denoting harmony]
- gathers people around him, not striving for special advantages for himself, but working to bring about general unity
- the power of persisting in time
- power does not show externally, yet it can move heavy loads
- he seeks nothing, asks nothing of anyone, is not enticed by dazzling goals [CC doesn't endorse a subservient relationship with humans]
- to rule is truly to serve

Understanding Key Terms

Our individual and collective ideas, our cultural and religious histories, necessarily inform our understandings until subjectively questioned and examined. This subjective questioning means allowing the Cosmic Consciousness to guide us in understanding the Cosmic Perspective of a situation or idea, which is often quite different from our assumptions and presumed beliefs. Attaining an understanding of this Perspective involves a journey that is an ongoing, developmental process and one that is directly fueled by our own interest and commitment to learning. Humans are capable of receiving this guidance by means that are relevant to our nature — such as intuition, intellect, bodily sensations, language and dreaming. "Energy renewing itself" refers to aspects of the Cosmic Consciousness that energetically flow through all living forms, not just human beings, providing each life form with the innate knowledge needed to function in and adapt to its environment. It is from this inherent capability that we are able to access the help that the CC actively provides to receptive learners.

As long-term users of the *I Ching* realize, this process of learning actually involves unlearning assumptions and viewpoints that we take for granted as correct or valid. Since human beings are creatures that rely heavily upon language, we come to our sessions with the CC from a particular frame of reference. The operative word here is "frame" because it means that our perspectives are necessarily limited or enclosed by whatever our cumulative experiences have been in life. Therefore, one of the major challenges people encounter in working with the *I Ching* is making sense of the metaphorical language. Throughout this book, and specifically within this Chapter, I will be sharing my experiences in learning from the CC the intended meanings of specific, commonly used words in the text.

Whatever metaphor the CC points to during an *I Ching* reading has a meaning that is applicable to the specific situation the person is addressing. Practical tips on how to discern these specific meanings will be discussed further in Chapter Four. Having said that, it is important to begin with a background understanding of the harmonious or intended meanings of key ideas and words that are often used in the text. This is important because when we realize the Cosmic Perspective of an idea or word, we then have an essential springboard from which to proceed in discerning the intended guidance that the CC is offering. Interpreting the text too literally or applying a common usage of a word can lead to obstructions in understanding that result in our completely missing the intended guidance.

Power

In the descriptive metaphors regarding the nature of the CC, there are many references to "power," which is a concept that is susceptible to misinterpretation if we relate to the term from the lens of conditioned beliefs. When the CC offers guidance that uses the term "power," it is often paired with the word "gentleness," underscoring the general principle that the CC does not use force in any capacity. Such a principle may seem counterintuitive because we often speak about "the forces of Nature" as powerfully destructive and frightening, but it is not referencing such forces. While the image of a "thunderstorm" indicates the idea of electrical energy, it does not refer to the violent display of such energy as we witness it in Nature, but to the gentle energetic penetration of influences from the CC to a human's consciousness.

There is frequent mention in the text of "the ruler" which, in some situations, may refer to the true self in position to lead a person. "He meets his ruler who is of like kind," refers to those aspects of the CC that are within each person. Other times, it may be a reference to the CC, though not in the sense of powerfully ruling over anything. With regard to this point, the CC has made it clear what its relationship is to human beings, from Hexagram 42 (Increase): *"To rule is truly to serve."* In the ultimate example of true modesty, the CC offers help to humans. It furthers everything through gentleness without encroachment, maintaining its own integrity while also protecting ours. Thus, it supports the protection and development of our true selves. In keeping with its integrity, it cannot further anything that is disharmonious. But it can and will restore harmony, as will be discussed in Chapter Five.

There are also some terms used in the *I Ching* that pertain to the cultural mores of ancient China that need to be adapted to a harmonious usage. For example, the many references to wars and battles may apply to the state of inner conflict of a person, or it may refer to disharmonious relationships among people. But, from a Cosmic Perspective, harmony does not involve intentional force, whether through action or simply within a person's thoughts or attitudes. This is because thoughts, feelings and attitudes are forms of energy and are transmitted whether we are aware of it or not. Because so much of the modern world operates on principles of force and power, it's easy to adopt disharmonious approaches without conscious awareness. But the CC can point out when this is happening and whether it is manifesting in our actions or intentions. This is important to identify when it is occurring because such energies can block a harmonious intervention for healing, as will be discussed in Chapter Five.

Soul

Hexagram 57 (The Gentle/Penetrating/Wind) points to how *"the ruler's thoughts should penetrate to the soul of the people."* The "soul," a term mentioned a few times in the *I Ching*, is being used by the CC to indicate human consciousness while in the form of a body. The energetic penetration of "thoughts" from the CC to an individual human being is one of the fundamental aspects of the teacher-student relationship we form with it. The CC also underscores that, in regard to this gentle penetration, *"time is its instrument"* in the unique, developmental relational process of learning. In Hexagram 55 (Abundance), it points to the phrase, *"the time of abundance is usually brief,"* to indicate our "brief" bodily lifespans within the context of eternity.

Water

There are other metaphorical patterns that illustrate the relationship between the CC and human beings in a general way, such as *"Heaven and earth are in contact and combine their influences"* (Hexagram 11, Peace). As living creatures on earth, humans are immersed within a *"teeming, chaotic profusion"* (Hexagram

3, Difficulty at the Beginning), but the "*chaos clears up*" after "*a thunderstorm brings release from tension and all things breathe freely again.*" We receive help as "*the wind disperses gathered clouds*" and "*subordinates itself in gentleness*" (Hexagram 57). The image of water is often used in reference to aspects of the CC, as well as human consciousness. It may also be used as a symbol for the nourishing relationship between it and humans. As in the above quote, the "thunderstorm," or one's relationship with the CC, can "release tension" from various forms of misunderstanding and suffering. "*Wind blowing over water*" (Hexagram 59, Dispersion) may be used to indicate the dispersion of beneficent influences of the CC in a person's life. Similarly, "*water collects in lakes upon the earth,*" may refer to the accumulated effects of the CC's influence. When distraught, doubtful or in a "*state of inner oppression*" (Hexagram 47, Oppression/Exhaustion), the CC may indicate "*the lake has dried up,*" or "*When the water has flowed out below, the lake must dry up and become exhausted. That is fate.*" "Crossing the great water" is a phrase that appears often in the *I Ching*, which refers to our connection with the CC as well as a connection with our true self. It can also be used to indicate the efforts we are making to overcome obstructions to inner harmony, or obstructions in our relationship with the CC. It waits for us to approach, because it is our decision and choice: "*The best water is only a potentiality for a refreshment if it is not brought up*" (Hexagram 48, The Well).

Gender and Hierarchy

Some words in the *I Ching* are disharmonious from a Cosmic Perspective if they are taken at face value. The most obvious example is the exclusive reference to the male gender, "he," which should simply indicate "one" or a person in general. The only reference to "woman" is in relation to a patriarchal standing, relating to the family or her husband. Similarly, notions pertaining to "masculine or feminine" energies do not have relevance. Numerous references are made to the "superior man" but these do not pertain to hierarchy. A "superior man" may designate either the CC or a person's true self, minus any notion of actual superiority to anything or anyone. An important aspect in developing a working relationship with the CC is exploring the various ideas and attitudes about "deities" and related concepts of authority learned from religions, family or teachers. Some of these ideas can be barriers to forming a trusting relationship with the CC, but perseverance will eventually clear them away.

There are many references in the *I Ching* to the "inferior man" or "inferior people," which designates the "ego" within a person or even a group. (I use "ego" simply as a term for false, conditioned ideas; it has nothing to do with Freudian terms of id, ego and super-ego.) The ego represents the accumulation of conditioned beliefs and attitudes that are disharmonious from a Cosmic Perspective, which will be discussed further in Chapters Two and Three. While these conditioned ideas, actions and attitudes ultimately create destruction and decay, it's important to not get caught up in viewing the ego in terms of something "inferior" in our nature.

Good and Evil

At times, depending on the situation, the CC may point to words such as "good and evil," or "right and wrong," when alerting us to examine false ideas that need to be identified and dissolved. Depending on the context, it may also refer to "love of the good," for example, when referring to a person's unity with the CC. When the term "evil" appears in the *I Ching*, it refers to the ego but minus the judgmental feelings usually associated with the word. If a person perseveres in learning from the CC, it is possible to gain insights into the Cosmic Perspective of acts committed by people that we regard as truly "evil" or destructive. In fact, a hugely significant aspect of learning from the CC, if intent on understanding the Cosmic Perspective of something, is centered on examining our conscious and even unconscious ideas about good and bad, sin and purity, guilt and blame, justice and punishment, as well as forgiveness and retribution.

Fate

Fate is another term that is frequently mentioned and easily misunderstood. It is important to carefully clarify the intended meaning if this comes up in an *I Ching* session. In my experience, it is not congruent with a Cosmic Perspective to regard fate as something predestined or unchangeable. Whatever difficulties we get into, help from the CC can eventually clear things up over time, once we have learned to relate harmoniously to the situation. If our "lake dries up" from a state of inner exhaustion or error, there is always an opportunity to renew ourselves and return once more to our efforts. It can be quite heartening when we're feeling overwhelmed to receive the specific counsel from Hexagram 47 (Exhaustion): "*A well-to-do man sees the need of the lower classes and would like very much to be of help.*" Again, the hierarchical language needs to be amended to simply read that the CC is fully aware of our difficulties and is willing to be of assistance to the struggling person.

Inner Truth

The process of learning from the CC includes questioning our assumptions about reality. Each session we engage in with the CC involves the potential for gaining insight into the "*inner truth*" (Hexagram 61) of any situation we are examining. This may include new insights about managing our feelings, understanding the motives of ourselves or others and learning to respond to challenging situations and people in more harmonious ways. The inner truth reflects the Cosmic Perspective. In order to align ourself with this viewpoint, we need to develop our capacity for receptivity: "*a heart free of prejudices and therefore open to truth*" (Hexagram 61). Usually, it takes time to comprehend this viewpoint. Just being willing to consider the possibility of another perspective is a significant step. Depending on how deeply ingrained a disharmonious belief or attitude is, we may need to revisit it multiple times until we have been able to truly see the ways in which it is false or harmful.

The inner truth also reveals the invisible or hidden state of a person's consciousness. This includes the unconscious motives, feelings, thoughts or intentions within ourself or someone else that pertain to the issue being examined. This is why it is not possible to judge a situation solely based on the outer appearances of a circumstance. If it is necessary for us to become aware of the hidden factors within a person's consciousness, the CC willingly helps us to understand what these hidden factors are and how we can harmoniously respond. This is always done within the context of a healing purpose — whether for ourself or others. Effectively using our consciousness for healing will be discussed further in Chapter Five.

Descriptors for the I Ching

As the CC is able to utilize the medium of *I Ching* metaphors, it is possible to discern how it regards the utility of the text itself. Below are some metaphors (brief quotes from the *I Ching*) that the CC has used to describe the *I Ching* text and a person's appropriate use of it:

- the Creative works through sublime success....furthering through perseverance
- concrete, man-made object
- without a move on one's own part, there's an outside intervention....at first, we cannot be sure of its meaning: is it rescue or is it destruction?
- even happy turns of fortune often come in a form that at first seem strange to us ... must greet the new turn with respect
- the beginning of all things lies still in the beyond in the form of

ideas that have yet to become real, but the Creative furthermore has power to lend form to these ... ideas.

- each step attained becomes preparation for the next; time is no longer a hindrance, but the means for making actual what is potential [a person's potential to free aspects of the true self by working with CC]
- their will is directed to what is great [commitment to breaking free from conditioning]
- clarity makes it possible to investigate the facts [using the *I Ching* to find inner truth]
- to bring about a time of abundance, a union of clarity with energetic movement is needed. Two individuals [CC and a person] ... are suited to each other, and even if they spend an entire cycle of time together during the period of abundance, it will not be too long, nor is it a mistake. Therefore one may go forth, in order to make one's influence felt; it will meet with recognition.

Obstructing Ideas

Rather than regarding the *I Ching* as an esoteric text, it can be used within a learning process that has everyday, useful applications, which is deeply valuable in and of itself. It may seem counterintuitive that such a deeply significant process of growth is accomplished without any human teacher, leader or guide: yet it is a process that can be learned entirely through our own experiences. *"Where an inner relationship exists, no great preparation or formalities are needed"* (Hexagram 45, Gathering Together). We are born with the capacity to relate with the Consciousness that created our consciousness. Developing our relationship with the CC does not require special knowledge or training, nor a "spiritual" outlook, or any other acquired trait. But we do need a certain degree of receptivity, willingness and perseverance.

Ingrained conditioned beliefs might create internal prohibitions to venturing forth on this journey. Some prohibitions might be based on received ideas from religious or spiritual traditions, disbelief about the actual existence of a "Cosmic Consciousness" or its interest in communicating with us, and fear of trusting something that we don't understand, including fantastical conjectures that we may get involved with something "evil." It's also not uncommon to project upon the CC any conflictual relationship we had with our parents or caretakers. All such obstructions can be overcome as the CC leads us through an individualized process of healing and release from all types of internal and external obstructions.

When we are in a "discussion" with the CC during an *I Ching* session, it will let us know in various ways when our conditioned ideas are influencing our perspective. For example, if feeling mistrust towards the CC, either consciously or unconsciously, Hexagram 38 (Opposition) may be given to alert us of this problem: "*As a result of misunderstanding, it has become impossible for people who by nature belong together to meet in the correct way.*" Or from the same Hexagram: "*Coming upon a sincere man, one fails to recognize him at first because of the general estrangement. However, he bites through the wrappings that are causing the separation. When such a companion reveals himself in his true character, it is one's duty to go to meet him and to work with him.*" The "duty to meet and work with him" refers to developing a willing relationship with the CC — and with our true self — so that we may fulfill our potential. Ideas related to literal "duty" or anything pertaining to force, pressure, obligation, or ritual only serve to block an authentic relationship.

Throughout the *I Ching*, references to working with a "superior man" can be a call to follow the leadership of our true self: the "*companion who reveals himself in his true character*" (Hexagram 38). It is my experience that learning to access our true self reflects an ongoing development: it's a gradual, step by step process in releasing ingrained, disharmonious ways of thinking, acting and feeling. An essential aspect of working with the CC through the *I*

Ching is becoming aware of times when these conditioned ways of thinking are blocking our understanding of the intended meanings of the Hexagrams, which is discussed further in Chapter Four. Becoming aware of these misunderstandings is a foundational aspect in learning how to become unbound from the constraints that falsely limit our lives. Freedom from these fixed ways of thinking and feeling is important not only because it can broaden our capacity to understand the guidance being offered, but ultimately allows us to move through the world more harmoniously. "Harmony" is not simply a nice goal to strive for or an abstract ideal. The ability to live in harmony, which the *I Ching* would propose is our natural or "original" state of being, minus all of our acquired conditioning, profoundly affects the ways in which we perceive and respond to events, how well our body functions and our ability to tap into the beneficent energies of the Cosmos. Disharmonious energies, whether manifested in our beliefs, attitudes or feelings, block the natural flow of harmonic energies that exist within ourselves and in the Cosmos.

When speaking with people who have been working with the *I Ching*, they often describe experiencing a deep sense of relief because they attained clarity about a difficult situation, dissolution of a particular inner conflict, or a new perspective on how to harmoniously respond to a troubling person or circumstance. A sense of relief is experienced due to resolution of the problem, but also due to the deep, gradual trust and feelings of support that comes from the interactive process that we engage in with the CC. This interactive process of receiving help is meant to be used to address any issue affecting the life of the learner. No issue is too minor nor too complex to be addressed. The CC can also guide us to examine the unacknowledged attitudes, beliefs and thoughts that we might not be fully aware of which are blocking us. Equally important, it can be helpful as a method for understanding dreams, such as those which may be reflecting an inner disharmony, or dreams where the CC is communicating something important to our consciousness, which is discussed further in Chapter Two.

Basic Approaches to Discerning Guidance

It bears repeating that consulting the *I Ching* is not a static phenomenon; it is a relational exchange between the individual and the CC, in that moment. However, difficulties in understanding the intended meaning of the text can lead to confusion and giving up on the learning process. Some people find the language in the book to be too metaphorical and obscure to make use of it. Or it may be regarded as an interesting historical document, poetic treatise or mathematical code that has little application to modern life. But, as discussed earlier, the imagery and metaphorical language is precisely what allows a unique and fluid meaning to be conveyed for each context or situation that is being explored in the moment by the questioner.

It is similarly a great mistake to treat any part of the *I Ching* text as conveying a single interpretation that applies to all situations. Each metaphor, phrase, or sentence in the text might be used to indicate multiple meanings, depending on the context of the specific situation being explored. (The exception to this is the reference to "water," which denotes consciousness.) Sometimes a particular phrase or sentence may be used in completely opposite ways in different contexts, such as when the CC is underscoring an idea that is patently false. The precise intended meaning can be ascertained in each particular situation by using the coins to ask yes/no questions, as in, "Do you mean ____?" In this way, it becomes a "living text" that responds to our conscious as well as unconscious mind, rather than a sacred book that should never be questioned. However, as will be discussed in detail in Chapter Four, asking yes/no questions should be done sparingly because when overused, it can lead to confusion and cause a blockage in communication with the CC.

The CC has the capability to help us learn what is needed at the time. It always respects our integrity, with a full understanding of whatever obstacles, fears, or roadblocks we are currently experiencing. This includes obstacles that we are not yet even cognizant of possessing, but are influencing us in harmful ways. It takes time and perseverance to gain greater clarity and trust in understanding how the CC communicates with us, and how it relates to our true self and ego.

Some people may try to achieve a shortcut in learning by asking another person to do an *I Ching* reading for them. But doing this completely misses the point because the person is essentially being robbed of all the benefits of an interactive relationship with the CC. We cannot have a relationship by proxy. Discovering our own, individual relationship with the CC is truly a gift and one that is unique for each person. It is a relationship that evolves, endures, sustains and nourishes. We are so often trained to believe that we lack the necessary resources, or simply feel insecure with a strange and unfamiliar process to embark on this journey. But it is precisely within this process of unfamiliarity that we learn to recognize the presence of something that is communicating with us, and which seems to be answering our very question or inner feeling, even if unexpressed. The only true misfortune is if we give up on this relationship. Chapter Four describes in further detail how to overcome the various obstructions that may occur in discerning guidance.

CHAPTER TWO

THE TRUE SELF

As discussed in Chapter One, I experience the *I Ching* as a metaphorical text that portrays the relationship between human beings and the Cosmic Consciousness (CC). Over the years, I have come to understand this relationship as an unalterable, inherent aspect of life because human beings are expressions of consciousness in physical form. At the most fundamental level, consciousness is a type of energy. It is through an energetic process that human consciousness is able to "communicate" with or actively relate with the CC.

Human beings across time, cultures, and religious traditions have employed different means to access and express this communication, whether through prayer, meditation or various forms of rituals. The potential gift of the *I Ching* is that humans can use their consciousness to interactively relate with the CC that chooses to communicate through the metaphorical language of the text. This means we can get "feedback" from the source as to whether we are understanding something correctly or not, for example. (As an experiment, I have tried to accomplish this using other texts, such as the Tao de Ching, but it was not successful, largely because it was not designed for this purpose.)

Concepts of Energy & Consciousness

I preface Chapter Two with this discussion of energy because a clear understanding of the "self" as a form of energy is paramount to relating with the energies of the CC and with all of life. What we conceive of as our "self" is, at the most fundamental level, energy that may change form but can never die or simply disappear. An obvious example of this is when we think of water as a substance that changes form, from solid to liquid or to steam, depending on external conditions. The CC often uses the metaphor of water when referring to aspects of itself, as well as to the true self in humans. *"Ground water invisibly present within the earth"* (Hexagram 7, The Army) speaks to the underlying presence of the CC in all living things, including within each human being. In dreams, the CC may appear as a vast ocean, waves at a shoreline or as a tidal wave.

Just as we know that energy may change form, but never simply end or disappear, the energy of our human consciousness is also continual, taking on the form of a body, then returning to its "pure energy" state after life in the body ends, in eternal repetition of these cycles. There are many metaphors the CC uses to describe the continuation of human consciousness, particularly in Hexagram 24 (Return): *"After a time of decay comes a turning point....The old is discarded and the new is introduced. Both measures accord with the time; therefore no harm results....The idea of RETURN is based on the course of nature.... Everything comes of itself at the appointed time."* The idea of human consciousness, prior to taking form in a physical body, is expressed in Hexagram 30 (Clinging/Fire): *"The mind has been closed to the outside world in sleep; now its connections with the world begin again."* This same Hexagram provides another metaphor for consciousness taking form in a physical body: *"Fire has no definite form but clings to the burning object."* "Fire" as the eternal consciousness, "clings to" or manifests within "the burning object," speaking to our temporal body. Our body is the physical expression of consciousness, until the time when it burns out or expends its energy in the human form, returning to its pure energy state. The cycles of transformation of energy is a continual process of evolution; thus the phrase, *"it makes no difference whether death comes early or late"* (Hexagram 30), meaning that our evolution is continual and always in motion, regardless of the length of time spent in the form of a physical body in any given lifetime.

All life forms have their own unique type of consciousness, or patterns of energy. Human consciousness, when in bodily form, manifests as the totality of our energy patterns: this includes energy that is expressed through our thoughts, feelings, attitudes, actions and dreams, as well as our physical body. All of these aspects of our consciousness operate as a functional whole, meaning that they are interrelated rather than separate. Our thoughts influence our body chemistry, for example. Becoming skilled in attaining a state of inner calm allows us to become more aware of the presence of energies within, such as physical sensations, subtle thoughts, and even insights. Sometimes, during a moment of relaxation, a sudden understanding or solution may come to mind. Or we may become aware of feelings of anger toward someone that we had been re-pressing. Becoming more aware of our energies is a crucial first step in self-healing. Increased awareness also means being able to make conscious choices about what we do with these energies, rather than thinking that they mysteriously come out of nowhere and are beyond our control.

Our consciousness is something that obviously we possess; it is "us" in our most fundamental nature. While in bodily form, our consciousness is malleable; that is, our thoughts, beliefs, feelings, etc. change throughout our lives. *How* these energy patterns are expressed ultimately falls within the domain of our own awareness and responsibility. They represent the crux of our working relation-ship with the CC through the modality of the *I Ching*. It is through our individual consciousness that we possess the ability to commu-nicate with the CC to receive direct help in this ongoing develop-mental process.

Concept of the True Self

The CC has pointed to particular metaphors that pertain to the true nature of human beings. Just as a seed is the beginning form and most fundamental part of a flowering plant, the "seed" aspect of our true nature is our unity with the Cosmic Consciousness. Hexagram 31 (Influence), describes this unity: "*Heaven and earth attract each other*" and "*This attraction between affinities is a general law of nature.*" Our true nature is referred to in the *I Ching* as our "true self." It is through our true self that we maintain our unity with the CC and can thereby sense what is harmonious in a given situation.

References to harmony and disharmony are prevalent throughout this book. Harmony is the basis for the "attraction between heaven and earth." Our "natural affinity" with the CC means that all humans have an inborn capacity to access the forces of harmony within themselves. This may seem doubtful, incredulous or even delusional when observing the harmful and destructive behaviors that some human beings exhibit. Nevertheless, regardless of how far people may become separated from their innate qualities, harmony eventually restores itself. We can see this principle operate in our own life whenever we engage in restoring harmony within ourself, which is one of the main functions of a relationship with the CC. This restoration of harmony affects every aspect of our well-being and the direction of our life. Our states of inner harmony also extends to our environment, allowing us to effectively use our consciousness for healing, as will be discussed in Chapter Five. The mechanism for affirming, re-establishing and restoring harmony is through our true self.

The true self is one aspect of our total consciousness. It is through experiences during our life in a body that our true self has the opportunity to evolve, and this evolution contributes to the state of humanity as a whole. It is within the nature of the true self to seek out experiences that will help us in our evolution.

Continuation of Consciousness
From a Cosmic Perspective, the nature of the true self can only

be understood within the context of our continuation of consciousness. In preparing this Chapter, the CC prefaced a discussion of the continuation of consciousness topic with three quotes from Hexagram 2, The Receptive: "*The horse belongs to earth just as the dragon belongs to heaven,*" and "*This symbol* [horse] *is chosen because the mare combines the strength and swiftness of the horse with the gentleness and devotion of the cow.*" The metaphor of the "horse belongs to the earth" is referring to a human being in bodily form. During life on earth, we need the qualities mentioned of "strength, swiftness, gentleness and devotion." These are qualities needed to accomplish something, which will be discussed momentarily. The third quote the CC highlights from The Receptive is: "*Just as the light-giving power represents life, so the dark power, the shadowy, represents death.*"

Next, the CC continues with the theme of death by pointing to quotes from Hexagram 63, After Completion: "*The transition from the old to the new time is already accomplished.*" This transition is described as, "*Water over fire: the image of the condition ... after completion.*" This simple metaphor is communicating an essential message. It relates to the previous discussion of the transformation of water under various conditions. For our purposes of understanding the *I Ching* metaphors, the element of water represents consciousness. We know that when a kettle of water is placed over a fire, the heat creates a transformation of energy into the form of steam, as mentioned in Hexagram 63. This image represents the transformation of our consciousness into the condition of a physical body. Hence the term, "after completion" of this transformational process. Next, the CC emphasizes, "*Do not throw yourself away on the world but wait tranquilly, and develop your personal worth by your own efforts.*" This quote is a warning against wasting an opportunity to evolve our consciousness through living a life that accepts false conditioning. It also underscores the quote, "*indiffer-*

ence is the root of all evil ... symptoms of decay are bound to be the result." Remembering that "evil" is a concept that does not exist within a Cosmic Perspective, it is being used here as a synonym for ego. Thus, this quote makes the point that the ego is "indifferent" to the existence of disharmony, whether within ourselves or others.

The CC points to one result of such indifference to disharmony when it next directed me to Hexagram 23, Splitting Apart: "*the bed is split up to the skin,*" referring to our separation from the true self. But as frequently emphasized by the CC, this condition of decay can always be reversed, depending on the choices we make in the effort: "... *the princess leads her maids-in-waiting like a shoal of fishes to her husband and thus gains his favor. Therefore all goes well.*" In this situation of splitting apart, the CC refers to the true self as the "princess" who is capable of leading the individual to reverse course ("like a shoal of fishes"), once again returning to harmony. The person then "gains favor with the husband" as a metaphor for unity with the harmony of life, whereupon "all goes well."

The CC began this particular discussion of the continuation of consciousness by pointing to some of the qualities needed in a person's life on earth, as identified in Hexagram 2, The Receptive: "strength, swiftness, gentleness and devotion." After the completion of our transformation following "death," our consciousness is in a place where "the transition from the old to the new time is already accomplished," as new life in a body. We must now "develop our personal worth by our own efforts" to combat any "symptoms of decay" or separation from our true self. To accomplish this, we need to utilize the qualities mentioned. Strength and swiftness speak to the capacity for making any needed reversals from disharmony. Gentleness and devotion speak to our approach to this task, by tempering our resolve to overcome the decay, with a true understanding for the mistakes we make along the way. Finally, the CC summarizes this task in Hexagram 14 (Possession in Great Measure), but makes an amendment to the language: "*Thus the superior man curbs evil and furthers good, and thereby obeys the benevolent will of heaven,*" is actually harmonious when it reads, "*Thus the true self curbs the ego and furthers one's evolution, and thereby follows the benevolence of harmony.*"

Descriptors for the True Self

Listed below are some other metaphors appearing in the text that describe the true self (TS) and its functions:

- a faithful steward who furthers the general welfare
- she is the treasure of the house [our TS as the "treasure" within our consciousness]
- attends to the nourishment of the family [TS is our source of nourishment through its connection with CC]
- it is the woman of the house [TS] that the well-being of the family depends
- leadership should come from the head of the family [TS as leader]
- when the family [our total consciousness] is in order, all social relationships of mankind will be in order
- cultivates the personality [deconstruction of false self] so it works through the force of inner truth
- does not permit thoughts to go beyond the current situation
- form is to be considered only as result of content [our bodily form is an expression of consciousness]
- influence on others must proceed from one's own person [responding to situations from the TS]
- ethical change is the most important increase of personality [becoming more in tune with our TS]
- develops so much inner strength, it acts as weapon against all that is false
- ground water stored up ["water" as metaphor for both CC & TS]
- efficient general who maintains obedience of the army, without strict discipline, nothing can be accomplished [learning to limit energies coming from the ego]

- it is not given to every mortal being to bring about a time of abundance [everyone is given free will or has a choice in whether they want to move towards freeing their TS]
- if an individual is careful and keeps his wits about him, he need not become alarmed or excited. If he's watchful, even before danger is present, he's armed when danger approaches and need not be afraid
- it is the business of the superior man to recognize when the time for retreat has come [learning to recognize and withdraw from conditioned impulses in self or others]
- restrains and tames [TS restrains emotions arising from conditioning; this is not the same as repressing feelings but refers to calming yourself so you can investigate issues]
- a man brings about real increase by producing in himself the conditions for it [another reference to undertaking the process of removing false beliefs]
- he does not lose touch with his inner being, finds a place of shelter in which he can stay [TS as safe and reliable "shelter"]

Our true self is the expression of harmonious energies within us. These energies can be validated and nurtured, or can become blocked and oppressed. Our ability to sense the helpful influences coming from our true self might shift, moment by moment. What allows us to become more receptive to these influences? How do we discern the voice of the true self from the voice of the ego? We should not allow anyone, especially our own ego, to imply that it cannot be done, or that it is too difficult to accomplish so don't even bother trying. These are skills that can be learned, possessions that can be developed. Clarity and strength are ultimately two of the most important possessions to develop and nurture. Clarity allows us to clear the fog so that we can recognize the presence of ego influences; strength allows us to gather the courage to reject these influences. Just as other animals in nature have been given innate abilities to sense danger in their environment, we are blessed with the capacity to sense disharmony, whether it is occurring within our own psyche or in our social environment. With practice, we can learn to become attuned to these innate abilities. The next crucial step is learning how to dissolve any disharmony, which can only be done effectively with the help of the CC. These steps are discussed in Chapters Four and Five. Actively engaging in this process of learning about harmony and disharmony is what the *I Ching* refers to as self-development. It is one way that our consciousness is able to evolve.

Choosing the Self That Leads

The true self (or true nature) has its origin from the Cosmic Consciousness. In contrast, the constructed self is the ego, which functions as an acquired false self. In a very practical way, learning from the CC through the *I Ching* is a way of becoming more aware of the ways in which the ego or constructed self blocks the expression of our true nature. This individualized education includes receiving guidance in how to nurture and develop the energies of the true self, while dissolving the disharmonious and destructive energies of conditioning that are influencing us. In doing this, we are evolving our consciousness.

The development or evolution of our consciousness is addressed in Hexagram 48, The Well: "*And every human being can draw in the course of his education from the inexhaustible well-spring of the divine in man's nature. But here likewise two dangers threaten: a man may fail in his education to penetrate to the real roots of humanity and remain fixed in convention—a partial education of this sort is as bad as none—or he may suddenly collapse and neglect his self-development.*" There are many references to water in this particular Hexagram, an element that appears throughout the text as a metaphor for the CC and its nourishing aspects. The water element can also refer to those aspects within human consciousness that are inherently connected with the CC. The "jug" or container mentioned in Hexagram 48 may be thought of as human consciousness in physical form. It is through our true self that we are able to access our inherent unity with the CC.

Learning about the nature of our true self and nurturing our connection with it is a choice we make in life. The "inexhaustible wellspring of the divine in man's nature" refers to the presence within us of the nourishing energies and influences from the CC. The text here warns of wasting our opportunities in life through failing to dismantle the constructed self. It refers to this failure as "two dangers" which are "remaining fixed in convention" and neglecting our "self-development." However, I don't see the "two dangers" in terms of either/or proposals because, for me, they are the same thing. Living our life within the fixed confines of acquired conditioning *is* a form of neglecting the development of the true self. In this situation, the true self remains a stranger. This means the CC also remains a stranger because the true self is our source of access to it: "*He is like a purified well whose water is drinkable. But no use is made of him.*" This misfortune is temporary, however, because each lifetime brings another opportunity. This same Hexagram invites us to consider the idea of the continuation of consciousness from one life in a body to the next, with the reminder that "*Life is also inexhaustible....The generations come and go, and all enjoy life in its inexhaustible abundance.*" Each lifetime holds opportunities to further our learning and to evolve our consciousness: "*It is only through repetition that the pupil makes the material his own*" (Hexagram 29, The Abysmal/Water).

The Basement Dream

The image of reaching into the depths of the water to "draw from the well," or accessing our connection with the CC, is expanded in Hexagram 48 through this advice: "*We must go down to the very foundations of life.*" A few years ago, I received an amazing gift that provided a deeper understanding of the meaning of this advice through the following dream:

~~~~~~

I am standing inside a very old building. I sense the presence of someone next to me. There is no physical or visual aspect involved with this presence: it has no gender, there's no light, no sound, no words spoken, yet we are communicating with ease. It points to an old dark staircase with rickety steps. I respond in quite an arrogant tone, "I'm not going down *there*!" But it simply turns on the light switch at the entrance to the staircase. It proceeds down the stairs and I follow. We soon reach an empty room that reminds me of a barn because there are remnants of fur and feathers on the floor. I think, "Oh, this is where they kept the animals." From here, another door opens. I look inside and see a dining room filled with people. Each person is sitting alone at a small table, waiting to receive a gourmet meal consisting of several courses.

~~~~~~

Over a period of months and then years later after this dream, the CC clarified and expanded upon the meaning: The "old building" and descending a "dark rickety staircase" represent the foundation of our existence, freed of the physical body. The fur and feathers in the room "where animals were kept" represents a "place" of transformation of human consciousness. It is during this place of transformation that each person's consciousness receives what is needed for evolution. The dining room where each person is waiting for the "gourmet meal with several courses," represents the individualized lessons designed to nurture the evolution of consciousness for each person in a particular lifetime.

In terms of the "Basement Dream," it is our choice how we

embrace the individualized courses in the pathway of our life. Those who seek help in this process of growth can always find guidance as needed. Some people neglect engaging in this process of growth, not because they are bad people, but because they lack understanding or awareness of the dangers of such indifference. The *I Ching* addresses the situation of a person neglecting the work of self-development, such as in Hexagram 53 (Development/Gradual Progress): "*The result is that relationships remain sterile and nothing is accomplished.*" The "sterile relationships" refers to being unable to relate to the CC. The loss of connection with the CC is also described in Hexagram 41 (Decrease): "*The lake at the foot of the mountain evaporates.*" The lake, as a body of water, represents the CC within our consciousness; our connection with it can become temporarily lost, or "evaporates." In a similar way, Hexagram 58 (The Joyous/Lake), warns that if people become "...*empty within and wholly given over to the world ....they lose themselves more and more, which of course has bad results.*" It also advises that when a lake has dried up, the person can find renewal through the CC: "... *when two lakes are joined they do not dry up so readily, for one replenishes the other.*"

Neglecting self-development can result in a loss of access to one's true self. If allowed to continue, this state may become a fixed way of being in the world. This means the constructed self is totally dominating the person, which may eventually be expressed in the most destructive of ways, such as suicide and homicide, as well as other forms of harmful behaviors. But it is always possible for someone to regain access to the true self, though no one can say if or when this might occur in a person. We need only be open to the possibility. Chapter Five discusses how we can learn to use our consciousness to set limits on these destructive energies, whether coming from ourselves or other people.

Dreams as Gifts

Another way to become receptive to influences from the true self is to pay attention to dreams. The ostensible notion that all dreams are merely brain neurons firing at random is an unfortunate belief that only leads to missed opportunities. An important part of our growth process is to work with the CC to verify which dreams are relevant and to seek its help to analyze them from a Cosmic Perspective. It is not helpful to rely on the idea of dream archetypes or set meanings for particular images because doing so would be a complete antithesis of the gift-nature that some dreams represent for the individual. One general exception to this interpretation guide-line is the metaphor of water which, in my experiences, represents influences of the CC.

There are particular metaphors the CC uses that represent different aspects of the phenomena of dreams. It refers to human consciousness during the sleeping state as, "*being nothing but air, without solid body,*" in Hexagram 9 (The Taming Power of the Small). In this same Hexagram, it describes the presence of the CC in our consciousness during the sleeping state as, "*wind blowing across the sky ... the rising breath of the Creative ... makes them grow.*" The presence of the CC is also expressed in terms of a rela-tionship between our subconscious mind and the CC in Hexagram 55 (Abundance): "*Two individuals ... are suited to each other, and even if they spend an entire cycle of time together during a period of abundance, it will not be too long, nor a mistake....Therefore, one may go forth, in order to make one's influence felt; it will meet with recognition.*" In this instance, the "cycle of time" refers to our sleep cycles. It represents a "period of abundance" because the CC can "make its influence felt" in a direct way that bypasses the inherent limitations of the intellect. It is the sensory aspects of our nature during sleep, freed from the confines of the conscious mind, which allow us to experience "the rising breath of the Creative." Such dreams can be a highly effective way for us to receive information that is foundational for our growth or progress. Once the imagery has been received, it provides a springboard for our beginning to investigate the lesson or issue that the CC is suggesting we address.

The imagery presented and the stories told in these dreams are often dramatic and vivid, and the energy of the dream experience may stimulate our bodily senses. These are dreams that are usually easy to recall, and the sensory stimulation may be consciously felt just as we are emerging from the sleep state. Obviously, it is important to record the dream soon after waking, while it is still fresh for recall.

The CC underscores the importance of making the effort to understand the dream's intended message. In Hexagram 55 (Abundance), there is encouragement to investigate how the dream relates to an issue in our lives: "*the ruler* [TS] *is modest* [receptive] *and therefore open to the counsel of able men. Thus he is surrounded by men who suggest to him lines of action. This brings blessings.*" This same Hexagram advises how to take full advantage of the potential gift it offers: "*To bring about a time of abundance, a union of clarity with energetic movement is needed.*" The "energetic movement" refers to the influence of the CC moving throughout our consciousness. We make a "union of clarity" by perceiving the inner truth of the dream with the help of CC. The gift of a Cosmic Perspective or inner truth that is being offered to a person is referred to as "*energy complemented by wisdom,*" and this applies whether the gift of this Perspective comes in the medium of a dream or during a session with the CC using the *I Ching*.

A few years ago, I experienced the gift of a dream about a friend. For a variety of reasons, we had lost contact for nearly a decade, yet she still held a very special place in my heart. The following dream speaks to how energetic connections in consciousness are not limited by time or space:

I am inside someone's house. Through a large window from inside the home, I see my friend standing outside, on the other side of the window. She waved to me and proceeded to walk back to where she came from. At that moment it began to rain.

It was not until two months *after* this dream that I discovered my friend had died; and that her death had occurred almost two months *prior* to my receiving this dream.

After I discovered that my friend had died (left her life in a body), I began to understand the true message of the dream. My heart was filled with a deep sense of blessing and gratitude for what I had received: the gentle and generous nature of the CC informing me of the transition from her living body, preparing my psyche even before I had consciously discovered the facts of her death; the affirmation that her consciousness was still active on some level; and the validation of our inner connection that transcended time and space. I perceive the element of water as representing the CC, so I felt comforted by the appearance of rain as she walked away, knowing that she was on her next journey within the Cosmic Consciousness.

Dreams may provide information we need in any situation, including seemingly mundane or practical matters. Some dreams have informed me of issues related to nutrition and vitamin supplements, and when a particular medical test was unnecessary, for example. On the other hand, the profound beneficence of the CC is demonstrated when we receive dreams that signal help is needed on behalf of another person. In this case, we can use our consciousness to facilitate healing, which will be discussed further in Chapter Five.

Attributes of Perseverance

The secret to achieving success on this path of learning is not in possessing some special talent or mystical wisdom: it is perseverance. In terms of receiving education directly from the CC through the *I Ching*, perseverance takes on many qualities. It is what allows us to keep moving forward despite any obstructions, misunderstandings and mistakes that may occur. Throughout this educational process, we are gradually "developing character" whereby we respond to situations differently— perhaps with more patience, wisdom, insight or strength to face problems that arise.

In my experience, perseverance in learning includes:

- willingness to be open to the possibility of a Cosmic Consciousness that communicates with us; it is only through repeated experiences that we learn to trust in its existence.
- accepting being a student of the Cosmos; not acquiescing to it, or belittling ourselves, but as an active participant in a relationship of mutual respect.
- returning again and again when discovering we have misunderstood its guidance, or made a mistake.
- willingness to repeatedly disengage from emotions that make the learning process difficult such as frustration, self-blame, anger, fear, self-righteousness, relentless striving, etc.
- learning the difference between true and false humility.
- dissolving the fear of trusting ourselves and looking to someone else to lead us.
- letting go of being the powerful one and using forceful means that we have been taught are "natural" and right.
- willingness to learn what the Cosmic Consciousness considers to be disharmony or force.
- accepting that expansion of consciousness entails learning from errors: this means retreating from paths that turned out to be mistaken, and discovering the false ideas that have been driving our decisions and feelings, without self-flagellation or embarrassment.
- paying attention to the subtle signs or synchronicities that the Cosmic Consciousness gives us throughout our life to guide us.
- working through each of the false requirements we imagine to

exist in life: such as attaining development to the point where we never again make any more mistakes, impressing the Cosmos with our perseverance, presuming a duty to save others or show them the correct way.

- devoting each part of the day to quietness, inner listening, feeling and communication with the Cosmic Consciousness.

Gaining access to our true nature has profound implications for maintaining well-being in all aspects of our lives. Bit by bit, our true self emerges as our source of influence, and we begin to feel the precious jewel that we hold. It is *"a time of blessing and enrichment,"* as described in Hexagram 42 (Increase): *"These persons become free of error, and by acting in harmony with truth they gain such inner authority that they exert influence as if sanctioned by letter and seal."* As will be discussed in upcoming Chapters, becoming "free of error" does not mean trying to attain a supposed state of self-perfection or complete freedom from influences of the constructed self. It means becoming skilled in dissolving any disharmonious energies that may arise so that our true nature can be expressed. In this way, we "gain inner authority." We become more attuned to perceiving what is harmonious from a Cosmic Perspective, or the inner truth of situations. Ultimately, this growth process means that we can effectively use our consciousness to "exert influence" for healing purposes, which will be discussed in detail in Chapter Five.

CHAPTER THREE

THE CONSTRUCTED SELF

Another aspect of human consciousness is our conditioned or constructed self, commonly referred to as the ego. The constructed self includes whatever disharmonious beliefs, attitudes, identities and experiences that we have acquired during a lifetime of conditioning from all sources including family, institutions, the media, etc. A key aspect of the insidiously harmful nature of conditioning is that these are accepted and expected ways of thinking and being that are so prevalent that we take them for granted as correct. They become ingrained as unconscious patterns that shape our perspective of life, sabotage harmonious relationships, disrupt the healthy functioning of our body and limit us from fulfilling our true potential. Conditioned beliefs may encourage us to unconsciously develop a false sense of identity that blocks or even overpowers our authentic, true nature. Conditioned beliefs can take over all aspects of life because we grow to rely on them as our point of reference for interpreting events and literally determine how we perceive and define "reality."

It is always our choice and our responsibility to determine how we will use our energies in the world. One of the main opportunities in working with the CC through the *I Ching* is to discover how our true self versus constructed self manifests in the expression of our personality, the choices we make, our values, feelings and ultimately our actions. On the surface, discussion of these "two selves" might seem as though we are dealing with dichotomies within our nature. Indeed, language within the *I Ching* often presents such dichotomous images, as will be discussed shortly. But from a Cosmic

Perspective, the CC makes it clear that while disharmonious energies may be present within our consciousness at any point, it is only our true self that is the core of our existence. The constructed self represents purely acquired energies operating within our consciousness that are superimposed upon or interfering with the expression of our true nature. Keeping in mind a clear distinction between the true and constructed self is of great importance in facilitating healing interventions, which will be addressed in detail in Chapter Five.

The *I Ching* text often depicts a battle for leadership between the "inferior and superior man," which represents conflict from the disharmonious energies that are blocking our true self at any given moment. As with some other metaphors used in the text, these are terms that need to be interpreted through the lens of a Cosmic Perspective, rather than in a literal sense. While the true self can represent the "superior man," it may at times also refer specifically to the Cosmic Consciousness. But, as previously discussed, the harmonious interpretation of this metaphor would not include notions of superiority or authority over anyone. Similarly, the inferior man or constructed self is not a "lower or evil" aspect of ourself; it simply represents the accumulated acquired conditioning in us that becomes energized through our giving expression to it.

We can make this disharmonious or constructed self grow stronger through whatever validates its existence: by the ideas we accept, the people we listen to and, most importantly, by the incessant voices of authority that we have unconsciously internalized. In the same way, we can make our receptivity to the true self grow stronger by understanding the forces that are blocking it. This is done most easily through a relationship with the CC, because the sources that can nourish our true self are internal or within our own consciousness, rather than external or within society. A partnership between the CC and human beings is expressed in Hexagram 42 (Increase) as the "*marriage of heaven and earth*." This partnership offers the potential for transformations: "*If great help comes to a man from on high, this increased strength must be used to achieve something great for which he might otherwise never have found the energy, or readiness to take responsibility.*" Accessing our connection with the CC is a pathway to discerning guidance and receiving the penetrating healing influences from the CC. Getting to know the nature of the true self, and the various ways that the conditioned self tries to overpower it, is a fundamental aspect of working with the CC.

Descriptors for the Constructed Self

Listed below are some metaphors appearing in the *I Ching* text that describe the constructed self and its effects:

- state of polarity [indicating the back and forth movement between the activity of the true self and constructed self]
- a dubious companion
- throws self away on unworthy friends
- a man's faults prevent well-disposed people from coming closer to him [as when access to CC is blocked]
- unreflecting, instinctive [automatic] way of acting brings misfortune
- heaven's will and blessing do not go with his deeds ["heaven" refers to a system of Harmonics]
- help gained by dubious fashion [false solutions offered by the constructed self]
- there are people of a certain instability who feel a constant urge to reverse themselves
- it is by no means a sign of courage or strength to insist upon engaging in a hopeless struggle [battling with the ego; obstinacy in pursuing ego goals]
- a man is in a society of inferior people [ego], but is connected spiritually with a strong and good friend [both CC and TS] and this makes him turn back alone [without the ego]
- when the time for return has come, he should not take shelter in trivial excuses, but should look within and examine himself

- making a boast of power leads to entanglements
- a powerful inferior in a high position who hinders deliverance
- designing foxes who try to influence the ruler ["ruler" may refer to either CC or TS]
- temptation to fall in with an evil element offering itself ["evil" as a reference to ego]
- seeks abundance and splendor for his dwelling; wishes at all costs to be master in the house and alienates the family [alienated from TS]; finds himself completely isolated [lost connection with the TS and CC]

We frequently hear the phrase, "that's just human nature," usually when referring to someone's negative behavior. It is a meaningless phrase, however, without specification: is it referring to a person's true self or to the constructed self? In my experience, that phrase most often is used as an excuse for accepting disharmonious behaviors because we assume they are "natural" or unavoidably part of our existence. Discovering the existence of the false self and deconstructing it is a life altering, freeing process. It is entirely possible to become freed from the arduous cycles of dissatisfaction, pain and defeat that inevitably come from following leadership of the constructed self.

Deconstructing various aspects of the conditioned self is the main focus in a working relationship with the CC. But a person might not come to the *I Ching* with this intention. The motive may be a problem that causes enough distress to seek alternative solutions. In the process of receiving guidance for the problem, the CC will help lead a person to discover the disharmonies within the conditioned self that are integral to the problem. We are helped to discover some of the sources for unhealthy patterns of thinking and behaving, which can include influences from one's immediate family as well as the accumulated effects from larger institutional and social forces. The CC refers to these sources of influence as "*the position of a man among rich and powerful neighbors*," referring to the pressures these influences can exert on us (Hexagram 14, Possession in Great Measure). In the following quote, "inferior and superior" refers to the constructed self and true self, respectively:

"In times of standstill it will happen that inferior people attach themselves to the superior man, and through force of daily habit they may grow very close to him and become indispensable ... Times of deliverance demand inner resolve. If he desires to be free of inferior people, he must first break completely free with them in his own mind" (Hexagram 40, Deliverance).

Suffering

The fact that we are often unaware of how such influential patterns exist and operate within us makes them difficult to identify and challenging to dissolve on our own. Realization that some of our accustomed ways of thinking and responding are disharmonious may come about through our own learning experiences in life as the obstacles created by these disharmonies become manifest. More often than not, these obstacles involve some form of suffering, which may in itself serve to stop us in our tracks and question. From a Cosmic Perspective, these can be valuable lessons if we are able to gain new insights or change harmful ways of being. In these situations, regrets may be felt, but ought not to become corpses that we carry around with us. Self-recrimination is merely another toxic pattern of conditioning. The psychic pain experienced from feelings of self-blame can be dissolved when realizing that the "mistake" which resulted in regret can be transformed by us into the means for becoming freed from one more hidden trap of conditioning within the constructed self. It is through learning from the error that allows us to breathe just a bit more easily, coming closer to our true self, and for this we can feel gratitude and relief.

But the Cosmic Consciousness has no desire for our suffering. The only designer of painful lessons is the enactment of disharmonious patterns which create natural consequences. But many of these conditioned patterns are often unconscious, thereby emerging as seemingly automatic responses in us. This lack of awareness makes it easy to place blame for the painful results on any variety of external factors, rather than recognizing harmful internalized patterns. And when a harmful action comes by the hands of another person, the CC can help us understand what the *I Ching* refers to as the "inner truth" or hidden aspects of the situation and how to deal with it in a way that does not bring further harm to ourselves or others.

Overcoming Suffering

We can interrupt any cycle of mental, emotional or spiritual suffering: first, by working with the CC in becoming aware of how our conditioned patterns are determining the way we're viewing the situation and second, by reformulating our viewpoint through gaining insight into the Cosmic Perspective of the situation. Each step in the process of gaining these insights involves unlearning something that we had believed was true, and transforms our feelings, attitudes and approaches to life.

"*If only the superior man can deliver himself*" (Hexagram 40, Deliverance) is quote that refers to our degree of receptivity as the main factor in being open to the transformational opportunity that awaits us in learning to understand the Cosmic Perspective. By discerning this Perspective, we can attain greater harmony within ourselves and our environment through the gradual process of dissolving the false conditioning that is the source of all human disharmonies in the world. "*When the family* [i.e., the consciousness within each individual] *is in order, all social relationships of mankind will be in order*" (Hexagram 37, The Family).

The "Receptive" meets the "Creative" when we acknowledge the need for a nourishment that is beyond ourself. Making this acknowledgement is in itself a large step if a person lives within a society or group that disparages seeking help from anyone other than human beings and their sanctified institutions. In this case, we might not seek help until we have exhausted all other solutions to an adversity that overwhelms all of our best efforts: "*He butts his head against the wall and in consequence feels oppressed by the wall. Then he leans on things that have in themselves no stability and that are merely a hazard for him who leans on them,*" as stated in Hexagram 47 (Exhaustion). It may be surprising and reassuring to the person in need who draws this Hexagram, to receive this reminder of a way out of the trouble in line 4: "*A well-to-do man sees the need of the lower classes and would very much like to be of help.*" Even though the CC would have us realize that it does not regard humans as inferior or "lower" beings, the descriptor of "lower classes" might mirror feelings of humiliation or embarrassment in seeking help, especially from a source that we are unsure of or may mistrust.

Because the constructed self becomes an integral learned aspect in our way of being and our identity, it may feel threatening to deconstruct it, or even to consider the possibility of another way of being. One of the many advantages of taking some time to live apart from society is that we are given the opportunity to be less closely tied to a socially constructed identity. When alone, relating only to our own thoughts and feelings and the Nature around us — if not filling up the spaces with media distractions, literature and phones — the usual reference points of social relations fade away. With no one to impress or defend against, no one to take care of or manage, no one to be the mirror for judgment or praise, we are free to discover what it means to live outside the framework of these socially constructed identities. Which can be a terrifying or disorienting prospect when separated from the familiar roles defined by gender, race, culture, religion, spouse, parent, profession, or any other category of social existence. To live without the boundaries of these categories is a freedom that many would prefer not to have. It is hopefully with compassionate insight if we come to realize that we have been choosing what is painfully familiar over the possibilities of the unknown. In this case, one of the first steps to positive change is to realize that we have developed into the prisoner who has become institutionalized and grown accustomed to the confines, restrictions, and dependencies of an incarcerated life, unable to live comfortably when freed — a type of recidivism as antidote to the terror of self-agency.

We may have been taught to seek a presumed safety through the socially sanctioned confines of these various roles. But we may later discover these are roles that turn out to be a perfect match for the job of masking particular insecurities. This does not mean giving up being a spouse, parent, caretaker, employee, boss, etc. It is identification with the role and our attachment to it that blinds us to the confining space it creates. The walls are built from the false assumptions, expectations and perspectives that have been assigned to the role. If the walls disappear — then what? I have to think for myself, make choices and be responsible for them, say no to others, risk ostracism and criticism, or do something for its own sake without recognition or visible outward success. Doing something out of fear, or not doing something out of fear; doing something to prove to others that we're not fearful; they are the same walls, eventually producing undercurrents of disappointment and dissatisfaction with life. Penitentiary or penthouse, ashram or hostel, suburban loft or cabin in the woods; you can never tell just by looking in the window if the abode is an escape from finding the true self.

Dismantling Inner Obstacles

Each experience in life provides an opportunity to gain insight into what comprises harmonious and disharmonious energy. Part of the task of the true self is to help remove whatever inner obstacles are preventing us from receiving all the benefits of living in harmony and fulfilling our potential. It takes time to learn how to identify these obstacles and to develop the strength needed to overcome them. In referring to this task, Hexagram 7 (The Army) reminds us that "... *he is equal to the heavy demands made upon him.*" The "demands" are the pressures from the constructed self, or from society in general. It is not possible nor are we meant to do this work completely on our own, without the aid of the CC. However, it is our responsibility to make choices about what thoughts, feelings, attitudes and actions we embrace because it is the harmony or disharmony in the energies we produce that determines the quality of our lives.

Responsibility means the ability to respond to the constant changes in our environment. A busy life filled with innumerable activities, obligations and duties, as well as the constant inner chatter of thoughts, can make us feel trapped, as if we have lost our freedom. Incessant activity can obstruct access to our true self, whether it is inner activity through thoughts, or outer activity through the unrelenting pursuit of goals. Yet it is our choice to exercise our freedom to interrupt these cycles of activity.

The first step in becoming receptive to our true self is creating a state of inner quiet. It is surprisingly easy to make momentary, regular withdrawals from outer activity and inner chatter, in any setting. First and foremost, it requires a simple decision to briefly stop whatever activities we are engaged in, close the eyes and sit quietly, even if in the midst of other activities going on around us. There are no special meditation techniques to learn, nor is a human teacher necessary. Learning to reach a state of inner quiet is a practiced skill that can be self-taught, such as simply focusing on movements of the breath, and daily increasing the few minutes of time in withdrawal from distracting thoughts and activities. It is not as though all distracting thoughts will disappear, but it is possible to become freed of their distracting quality. This can be done in many ways, such as imagining these thoughts simply floating down a stream. We can allow them to pass by the landscape of our mind, without getting involved in them through our attention. Even feeling upset that these thoughts are appearing is a form of attention that can take us off course. By this daily practice, a calmer inner state eventually becomes integrated within activities of daily living and we are better able to recognize when we have become separated from this state, particularly during an *I Ching* session. Practicing this type of withdrawal does require an initial commitment to ourselves because the pressures and temptations to be externally-focused are great. But in a short time, this practice becomes a self-reinforcing habit because it feels good. We don't need to force this process or develop a driven energy around it. All that is needed is a consistent withdrawal from the distractions so that a calm state can emerge naturally, without anxious effort. Mastering the ability to attain inner quiet allows greater access to the true self so that it can become the leader in our lives, rather than just making a glimpse appearance.

Once a state of inner quiet has been attained, we can begin to explore the obstacles that are creating problems in life through the guidance of the CC in using the *I Ching*. This exploration includes understanding the nature of the disharmony, removing it from our consciousness and healing any misfortune that had been produced. The CC leads us through this exploratory and healing process. Simply through our willingness to engage with it, guided by the voice we learn to listen to, we allow a pathway to open. *"The light-giving power begins to manifest,"* as described in Hexagram 1 (The Creative) and *"the great man makes his appearance."* What occurs here is the "appearance" within our consciousness of both the CC and our true self. It is from this basis that we can begin a step by step process of deconstructing the conditioned beliefs and attitudes in our psyche that are causing problems. This is discussed further in Chapters Four and Five. The results of this important work are described in Hexagram 15 (Modesty): "*the superior man ... establishes order in the world; he equalizes the extremes that are the source of social discontent and thereby creates just and equable conditions.*" It is the CC that creates order in the world, through individual human beings taking responsibility for their own disharmonies, thereby creating greater harmony within themselves. It is from this point that persons with sufficient experience can, when called upon, participate in the CC's healing the disharmonies within other people and situations, which is discussed in greater detail in Chapter Five.

Collapsing the Tyrant

One of the greatest assets in pursuing an education with the CC is gaining the ability to recognize the ego or conditioned self. In the process of deconstructing ego conditioning, we get to intimately know the many nuances, hidden voices and sneaky tactics that have taken up residence in our psyches. Recognition is a crucial key weapon in becoming freed from its hold because we can then clearly see it for what it is: "*a powerful inferior in a high position who hinders deliverance*" (Hexagram 40). We begin to see how "*the ringleaders of disorder*" repeatedly create havoc. We also can become skilled at recognizing when we backslide in the return of old habits, as Hexagram 24 (Return/Turning Point) describes: "*there are people of a certain instability who feel a constant urge to reverse themselves.*"

There are a few places where the *I Ching* directly mentions the ego. Hexagram 59 (Dispersion) speaks of "*the dispersing and dissolving of divisive egotism;*" Hexagram 15 (Modesty) states "*Genuine modesty sets one to creating order and inspires one to begin by disciplining one's own ego;*" and Hexagram 20 (Contemplation) offers "*Liberated from his ego, he contemplates the laws of life.*"

However, there are far more frequent references to the ego that are metaphorical, and it is helpful to be able to recognize them to understand the guidance of the CC. Hexagram 36 (Darkening of the Light) is devoted to addressing the constructed or conditioned self. It describes situations when the ego is *"in a position of authority,"* thereby creating conditions in which there is a *"wounding of the bright,"* referring to blocking the true self. This Hexagram counsels a person to have *"steadfast spirit when overcoming adversity,"* speaking to the perseverance needed to overcome disharmonies within ourselves and the consequences these disharmonies have produced in our lives. This Hexagram also mentions that *"While the strong loyal man strives eagerly and in good faith to create order, he meets the ringleader of disorder."* In one application, the "strong loyal man" can refer to the CC, faithful in its relationship with human beings, and ever-present in our ongoing evolution of consciousness. In another application, it can refer to a person who is on the path of discovering the true self, who "strives eagerly and in good faith to create order" within, but encounters the ego, the notorious creators of disorder within oneself and the world. A person's ego conditioning may at times cause a "total eclipse" that blocks receptivity to influences from the CC, as well as from the true self: *"The ruler is overshadowed by a party that has usurped power"* (Hexagram 55, Abundance).

As described earlier, "inferior man" refers to the ego in a person and "superior man" refers to the true self. When the CC wants to make us aware that conditioned viewpoints or attitudes are dominating, we may receive this line from Hexagram 43 (Breakthrough/Resoluteness), *"Even if only one inferior man is occupying a ruling position in a city, he is able to oppress superior men,"* or from Hexagram 7 (The Army), *"it is important that inferior people should not come to power."* The nearly constant exposure to societal conditioning means that we must make choices about what path we follow, as counseled in Hexagram 56 (The Wanderer): *"the wanderer should not demean himself ... with inferior things he meets along the way."*

It may happen that ideas absorbed from various religious, philosophical or spiritual traditions create biases in how we interpret the guidance offered. For example, a line from Hexagram 1 (The Creative) is easy to misconstrue if taken literally: *"free choice can enter in.... he can soar to the heights ... or he can withdraw into solitude to develop himself. He can go the way of the hero or that of the holy sage who seeks seclusion."* While a certain amount of time alone is needed for activities such as consulting the *I Ching*, meditating, reflecting, or journaling, a "life of solitude" is certainly not necessary. It is precisely our interactions and relationships with others that may become an important context for learning how to distinguish between our constructed and true self. It is through these interactions that we may come to examine our actions and what we believe to be correct; or judgments about ourself, another person or situation; or conclusions formed about events and what we think should have happened. "Soar to the heights" actually may refer to times when a person is totally immersed in some form of egotism, as described in Hexagram 36 (Darkening of the Light), *"With grandiose resolve, a man endeavors to soar above all obstacles."* The inner light of our true self can become obscured when we apply an egotistical solution to get out of a problem, and later find that it has only made things worse. In such cases, this same Hexagram counsels, *"In order to escape danger, they need invincible perseverance of spirit and redoubled caution in their dealings with the world."*

The metaphorical battle between the true self and the constructed self is a major theme within the *I Ching* text. It speaks of bloodshed, danger, blame and misfortune, which is as relevant for our current times as it was thousands of years ago when the *I Ching* was written. There are many references to *"the power of inferi-*

or people is growing," as mentioned in Hexagram 23 (Splitting Apart). It continues with "*the danger draws close to one's person ... and rest is disturbed ... disaster affects not only the resting place but even the occupant.*" The use of the term "disaster" should not frighten the reader: such extreme language in the context of deconstructing the ego simply refers to the disharmony it creates, such as anxiety, depression, and confusion. Certainly, long term effects of disharmony may create complex problems in life. But there is no problem that it is too difficult or complicated to be addressed with the CC. Perseverance in partnership with the CC eventually leads to deliverance. In this same Hexagram, we see that it is possible to "split apart" from the hold that the ego has on us: "*It no longer opposes the strong principle by means of intrigue but submits to its guidance....The seed of the good remains....The superior man again attains influence and effectiveness.*" These metaphors refer directly to one's true self gaining influence and effectiveness in subduing the ego, creating another victory in overcoming an ingrained pattern.

In our zeal to become freed from the tyrant aspects of conditioning, we may be reminded in Hexagram 40 (Deliverance) that "*the struggle must not be carried on with the wrong weapons.*" Such "wrong weapons" might include falling into a habit of guilt, anger and self-recriminations, when feeling stuck in the process of overcoming an ego obstruction. It is especially easy to pull out the wrong weapons when addressing a problem that requires time for healing to manifest externally. The voice of ego may try to present itself as the voice of reason and declare that surely too much time has passed. It may self-righteously demand visible results. Frustration, doubt and impatience are reactions that can easily take control if not held in check by the true self. It is the mistaken viewpoint imposed upon us by the constructed self that create these states of suffering. This is problematic not only because of the resulting emotional distress, but also because of the very real danger created if it leads to self-defeating actions in an attempt to relieve these painful feelings. Throughout the deconstructing process, we need to rely on the help of the CC in disentangling each thread of faulty logic and each assumption that supports a self-righteous assertion. Once exposed to the light of true perception, these disharmonious elements deflate as quickly as a popped balloon. Each time the Cosmic Perspective is ascertained, another step of progress is made in becoming freed. Chapter Four is devoted to discussing how to be open to the Cosmic Perspective and the ways the constructed self may interfere with this learning process.

CHAPTER FOUR

HEAVEN MEETS EARTH: AN APPROACH
FOR FELLOWSHIP

The *I Ching* represents a potential experiential dialog between human beings and the intelligent, energetic forces of universal harmony, as Cosmic Consciousness (CC). The *"universal mutual attraction"* between the Cosmic Consciousness and human consciousness is a *"persistent, quiet influence"* as described in Hexagram 31 (Influence/Wooing). Through the existence of this ever-present hidden stimulus, *"Heaven and earth attract each other and thus all creatures come into being."* Learning to consciously, intentionally relate with this invisible source of "influence" is conveyed in several Hexagrams as a type of courtship. It is a dance, a partnership of movement involving our intellect, intuition and senses. This courtship is marked by unlimited forbearance for our skepticism. In the midst of some life struggle, a dream appears: I am on the dance floor when approached by a very short man offering to cut in. I disparagingly think, "How is *he* going to be able to lead me?" But he smoothly and expertly guides me across the dance floor.

It is ultimately always our choice about who and what we allow the sources of influence to be in our lives. Hexagram 53 (Development/Gradual Progress) expands on the metaphor of influence and courtship as gradual growth: *"The development of events that leads a girl's following a man to his home proceeds slowly."* This emerging partnership cannot be forced; it develops over time as we build trust and confidence. Hexagram 54 (The Marrying Maiden) describes the beginning stages of our learning to relate with the CC: *"The marrying maiden is given in marriage."* A "maiden" represents someone unattached, such as the person not yet aware of the possibility of this relationship. The "marriage" consists of becoming loyal to the expansion of such an alliance. The developmental aspect of this relationship is alluded to by, *"Man and wife ought to work together like a pair of eyes."* We can disregard the patriarchal language to focus on comprehending how the CC is using the metaphor of "a pair of eyes." In a working relationship with the CC, we learn to move away from viewpoints that are misaligned or in conflict with harmony. We slowly move toward awareness of a Cosmic Perspective, just as "a pair of eyes" are aligned to move in the same direction. Sometimes the disharmonious beliefs and attitudes that we have internalized over time cause us to become separated from our true self and the CC: *"Here the girl is left behind in loneliness,"* as we feel the void from this separation. But the CC is always available to us, giving us the freedom to approach: *"Outwardly this man must keep tactfully in the background behind the official minister of state, although he is hampered by this status ... he can nevertheless accomplish something through the kindliness of his nature."* In this case the "official minister of state" refers to our subconscious mind; the CC might make its presence felt in our dreams, or remain "in the background" of our consciousness until we intentionally choose to approach.

The *I Ching* often speaks of "crossing the great water" and "accomplishing something" as metaphors for the life process of dissolving the disharmonies that trap our lives and separate us from our true nature. While this entails our own efforts, we are continually offered guidance, as expressed in Hexagram 46 (Pushing Upward): *"... there is a spiritual affinity with the rulers above, and this solidarity creates the confidence needed to accomplish something."* Hexagram 42 (Increase) offers similar encouragement: *"If great help comes to a man from on high, this increased strength must be used to achieve something great for which he might otherwise never have found energy, or readiness to take responsibility.*" It is through the slowly developing relationship of trust and confidence with the CC that allows us to move forward in this journey. Despite the hierarchal language within the text, such as "rulers," the forces of harmony actually support our movement toward independence, rather than reliance on any external system, organization, person, philosophy or edict.

Establishing an energetic connection with the Cosmic Consciousness represents the most effective use of our consciousness that is possible. It is through this connection that we can learn to 1) increase access to our true nature, 2) identify and dismantle the constructed self, and 3) become more aware of what comprises harmony and disharmony from a Cosmic Perspective, all of which are ways that further the evolution of our consciousness. This is a profound undertaking, described in Hexagram 49 (Revolution) as, "*Thus the superior man sets the calendar in order.*" This sentence refers to the true self (in this case, the superior man) possessing the ability to undertake a change (set in order), and "calendar" alludes to the idea of time (the eternal). The fact that this sentence is situated within the Hexagram of "Revolution," suggests that major undertakings of transformation are being addressed, namely, the evolution of consciousness. This seemingly abstract or esoteric point actually has practical applications to daily life that can become quite evident when putting into practice what has been learned in one's relationship with the CC. In order for transformations to be successful, a person needs to first have a thorough understanding of what comprises appropriate limits from a Cosmic Perspective. This point of working with appropriate limits to create transformations is discussed in detail in Chapter Five.

Descriptors for the Relationship Between the Cosmic Consciousness & Humans

The energetic connection that we form with the CC is not something that we can control or try to make appear; but we can remove whatever temporarily blocks our access to this natural affinity, and it thus arises on its own. There are many forms of advice in the *I Ching* for how to access this energetic connection, such as "keeping still" (Hexagram 52), or "quieting the movements of the heart." We are reminded that experiencing our natural affinity with the CC, and communicating with it through the *I Ching*, is a possibility open to the ordinary person, as echoed in Hexagram 45 (Gathering Together): "*Where inner relationships exists, no great preparation and formalities are necessary.*"

Listed below are some metaphors describing the relationship between the Cosmic Consciousness and human beings:

- a superior man joins with friends for discussion and practice [as discussed earlier, this should not be interpreted as a superior-inferior relationship between the CC and humans]
- when a man meets his destined ruler [replace "ruler" with CC as friend, teacher, confidant, companion, ally; "ruler" can also refer to discovering the true self as one's own leader]
- will feel sheltered in love
- marriage of heaven and earth
- when an obstacle to union [with CC] arises, energetic biting through brings success
- a heart free of prejudices and therefore open to truth
- many differences and obstructions arise, causing grief....but they remain true to each other, they allow nothing to separate them and though it costs them a severe struggle to overcome obstructions, they succeed [recovering the inborn inner connection humans have with CC]
- those who are uncertain or hesitant gradually come of their own accord
- he invites none, flatters none; all come of their own free will.

In this way, there develops a voluntary dependence among
those who hold to him. Police measures are not necessary, they
cleave to their ruler of their own volition

- if a man cultivates within himself the purity and strength necessary for one who is at the center of fellowship, those who are
meant for him come of their own accord. They do not have to
be constantly on guard, but may express opinions openly ["purity" pertains to efforts to break free from ego conditioning]

It takes time to establish a type of working relationship with the
CC where we are open to questioning our assumptions and willing to examine our motives, attitudes and behaviors. The purpose
of this examination is described in Hexagram 20 (Contemplation/
View): "*This self-contemplation means the overcoming of naïve
egotism in the person who sees everything solely from his own
standpoint....However, self-knowledge does not mean preoccupation
with one's own thoughts; rather, it means concern about the effects
one creates.*" Contemplation involves a sincere and effective form
of self-critique for one purpose only: to understand what is harmonious, what is disharmonious and why. It is not for the purpose of
self-perfection, purification, pleasing the Cosmos, superiority over
others or to attain an imagined reward. We might be reminded by
the CC that our "*resolve to choose the good brings its own reward*"
(Hexagram 24, Return/The Turning Point). But forming the inner
resolve to "choose the good" or becoming aligned with harmony is
an ongoing course. Through being consistently open to guidance,
we can learn what is harmonious from a Cosmic Perspective, rather
than blindly following imposed rules, commandments, precepts
or societal expectations. In concrete terms, this means relating
to ourselves, others and our environment in ways that are free of
disharmony, which is what ultimately affects every aspect of our
well-being. It is what enables us to move toward expressing our full
potential.

Self-critique is ultimately a process of gaining inner freedom.

It becomes an honest yet gentle method of learning with the CC. It includes examining ourselves and others with deeper insight and compassion. It involves gaining awareness of the conditioned beliefs that unconsciously drive behaviors. In this way, compassion is developed for others who are caught up in disharmonious actions, through the realization of how difficult it can be to unlearn conditioned ways of being, as we remember our own challenges in these efforts. It is not synonymous with forgiveness nor with excusing behaviors, which will be discussed further in the next Chapter.

Inner Independence

Learning how to discern guidance from the CC using the *I Ching* is necessarily a subjective endeavor. It involves intuitive sensing combined with intellect, and applying these capabilities in systematic ways through our experiences. We tend to disparage subjectivity as a form of knowledge because it is presumably "only our own opinion," as though our experiential knowledge of the world is divorced from all validity. Discernment and assessment are survival skills that we use in everyday life. Developing and refining these skills involves an emerging self-reliance that the *I Ching* refers to as "*inner independence*" (Hexagram 61, Inner Truth). It means we regard our own opinion about what we should do as more valid and relevant than what other people say we should do, which is eloquently expressed in this Hexagram as "*the root of all influence lies in one's own inner being.*" This quote is not referring to our trying to influence others, but rather how and by what criteria we allow ourselves to be influenced. It doesn't mean we're closed off to information from others, but we evaluate that information from the lens of what we've learned and experienced as harmonious. We become accustomed to seeking clarification from the CC of the "inner truth" of a situation, which reveals hidden aspects of consciousness relevant to the situation. This means understanding the current beliefs, attitudes or motives influencing ourself or another person that lie beneath surface appearances. It is from the perspective of inner truth that we formulate our assessments and actions, rather than from the opinions, judgments and statements from experts, leaders, and purported influencers, or from assumptions we make based upon external appearances of "reality." Because so much of the world chooses to operate by principles that are inherently disharmonious, we might begin to find that our harmonious choices, attitudes and actions differ from the status quo, or from expected behaviors. This does not necessarily mean that we would come into conflict with family, friends or associates — quite the opposite — because we can learn to use our consciousness to create more harmonious environments, which will be discussed in detail in Chapter Five.

Inner independence ultimately means that we allow our true nature to become the authority in our own life, rather than believing we need someone else to lead us to ready-made answers. The CC, in its provision of guidance, does not encourage servility toward it, and it does not support our trying to turn it into an authority over us. This concept of allowing our true self to become the "ruler" of our personality is described in Hexagram 37 (The Family) as, *"In a ruling position one must of his own accord assume responsibility."* The CC promotes our movement toward inner independence by helping us to strengthen the connection with our true self as the leader of ourselves. Just as it respects our space to learn, we respect the learning process of others, which includes not assuming that what is correct action for us in a given situation should be correct for everyone else. From my experience though, I would say that the most important aspect of inner independence is learning to discern and follow the voice of the true self instead of the insistent voices of internalized conditioning.

Practical Guidelines for Consulting the *I Ching*

In the remainder of this Chapter, very specific and pragmatic aspects of conducting *I Ching* consultations are addressed. In a sense, it seems odd that such specificity is applied to a process that is imbued with mystery and grace. But, practicality need not preclude grace. Anyone modest enough to approach the forces of harmony within and without will experience unique gifts that are inherently meant for one's individual journey in life. That such gifts may be experienced by others is my sincere wish. It is in this spirit that these guidelines are offered, gleaned from nearly four decades of working with the *I Ching*. I emphasize the years that I have invested not to highlight my authenticity and perseverance — though these do apply — but more pointedly, to help others embarking on this path to avoid some of the difficulties and obstacles I have faced in my long and still ongoing process of learning. The truth is that even though overcoming these obstacles has been useful for my growth, no one wants or needs to endure confusion. So anything that might clear a pathway for others is hopefully utilized in productive and encouraging ways.

Focusing the Session

Every consultation with the Cosmic Consciousness using the *I Ching* needs to begin with becoming centered. If experienced in meditation, then it might take only a few minutes to clear the mind of distractions and achieve a state of inner quiet. If the session is a long one, then it may be necessary to regain a state of being centered if distractions and loss of focus interrupt the session. The CC does inform you when focus has been lost or the ego-mind is interfering during a session, sometimes through a Hexagram that specifically mentions this, such as Hexagram 52 (Keeping Still) or Hexagram 38 (Opposition).

After a Hexagram has been received, it is possible to focus or streamline the guidance process by asking the CC "yes/no" questions to determine what sections of the Hexagram apply to the current issue. This means assigning a value of either yes or no to heads and tails of the coins (or obverse and reverse); it does not matter which designation is assigned, as long as consistency is maintained. This allows for a more accurate understanding by avoiding reading parts of the Hexagram that might lead in the wrong direction in terms of the message that the CC is trying to provide in the moment. Traditionally, six and nine were designated as changing lines, meaning that they would lead to a second related Hexagram. However, this practice is not needed because it is possible to ascertain more directly what the intended meanings are for any section of a Hexagram. If one or more lines in a Hexagram are involved, then you can simply begin by asking if there is anything that needs to be read before addressing the designated lines. If so, you can begin a process of elimination and start by asking if there is anything in the first paragraph of the Hexagram that applies, and so on for each section, until you reach the relevant lines being discussed.

The process that has worked for me is to read the identified section or line to feel what resonates. After reflecting, I verify if my interpretation is accurate by asking something like, "Are you saying _____?" If the answer is negative, then I proceed with a process of elimination to determine which sentences in the paragraph or line are relevant. Sometimes just part of a sentence applies, or even just one word. It is important to remember that the same word, image or phrase that is being underscored can obviously have different meanings across sessions, depending on the issue involved. For example, guidance from Hexagram 13 (Fellowship With Men) may pertain to your relationship with the CC, your true nature, or with another person. One exception to the flexibility of meanings that I have found is that references to water pertains to the CC or human consciousness. As with all interpretations of guidance, verification of the intended meanings can be ascertained by asking direct yes/no questions, but always combined with Hexagrams.

Challenges in the Partnership Journey

Everyone has a unique relationship with the CC, suited to the individual needs of the person. Yet there may be common experiences on this journey that create obstacles to an ongoing harmonious connection with the CC. The beginning formation of our relationship with the CC is described in this excerpt from Hexagram 4 (Youthful Folly): *"In the time of youth, folly is not an evil. One may succeed in spite of it, provided one finds an experienced teacher and has the right attitude toward him. This means, first of all, that the youth himself must be conscious of his lack of experience and must seek out the teacher."* Whether a beginner or longtime practitioner with the *I Ching*, there are numerous obstacles that can block, distort and limit our relationship with the CC. As described in Chapter Two, any obstructions that we are facing can be overcome through perseverance in the educational process with the CC. The only true danger in this path of learning is that we give up on ourselves and the CC.

We might receive heuristic messages from the *I Ching* that suggest internalized conditioning is blocking understanding of the current guidance: *"The power of inferior people is growing. The danger draws close to one's person....caution is necessary in this isolation"* (Hexagram 23, Splitting Apart). When a false, fixed idea is obstructing access to our true self or with the CC, we might also receive guidance such as this from Hexagram 17 (Following): *"In friendships and close relationships an individual must make a careful choice. He surrounds himself either with good or with bad company; he cannot have both at once. If he throws himself away on unworthy friends he loses connection with people of intellectual power who could further him in the good."* The "bad company" and "unworthy friends" are the familiar companions of conditioned beliefs which interfere with following what "people of intellectual power" would advise, namely, the CC and our true self. It should be noted that the CC also does not "throw itself away" or compromise its own dignity by acquiescing to intrusive demands from the ego. In such cases, we might receive a reminder such as, "*What is not sought in the right way is not found*" (Hexagram 32, Duration). Other reminders to follow our true self by "parting company" with the ego are revealed in Hexagram 11 (Peace): "*Make your commands known within your own town.*"

These reminders do not mean that the CC won't help us: the assistance offered is always in the form of furthering our strength and development so we can become more receptive to the inner wisdom of our true nature. But it might not appear that way to the constructed self, whereby it may launch all manner of opposition and an intense assortment of complaints and pleas. There is no set response that the CC gives in such situations, as the forces of harmony offer help in a variety of ways best suited for our understanding at the moment. A major factor in perseverance is returning to seek guidance, after we have calmed down and are able to listen with a clearer heart and mind. Should we seek to place blame on someone in these instances, we might be reminded that, "*When the time for return has come, a man should not take shelter in trivial excuses, but should look within and examine himself*" (Hexagram 24, Return/ The Turning Point). The CC doesn't hold these outbursts or misunderstandings against us and is always willing to be of assistance again and again, as we take a step forward in trusting the true self, and then backwards in falling prey to ego voices. Then the CC may give this friendly reminder — one of my personal favorites which always brings a smile: "*There are people of a certain instability who feel a constant need to reverse themselves*" (Hexagram 24). Eventually we learn that blame, guilt or judgment directed at ourself or others are destructive and irrelevant concepts in the context of our evolutionary growth process.

Dichotomous Questions

It is important to understand how to effectively use the system of asking dichotomous (yes/no) questions for clarification of guidance. Obviously questions need to be asked that are also dichotomous, meaning they can be answered only with a yes or no. A double-ended question cannot be answered; it must be split into two or more separate questions.

If a series of "no" answers are received, either in the beginning or during a session, then the cause needs to be identified, rather than giving up on the session. This is easily done by identifying the variety of possibilities such as, "Does no mean that I need to center myself?" You continue through a process of elimination until you reach an affirmative answer as to the cause. In my experience, a series of no answers could mean that the CC wants to initiate communication with a series of Hexagrams, before asking questions about an issue. This often occurs at the start of attempting to interpret a dream. In any session, asking clarifying questions prematurely can close off or limit the guidance the CC is trying to provide.

Sometimes during a session, I might get a sense of the meaning for something that the CC has underscored in a Hexagram, but receive a "no" answer when I propose my interpretation. At that point, I go through the procedure of elimination to determine if I am asking questions prematurely, which means that the CC is trying to provide a background for understanding the issue. The process feels somewhat like a painting whose colors and shapes are slowly arising to the surface of the canvas. At times, the complete scene might not emerge in that session. Depending on the complexity of the issue, or on our own level of preparation, the meaning of the guidance might not emerge until a few days later as our consciousness has had time to reflect. Comprehending the Cosmic Perspective of a situation is not a static or rigid process; it is important to allow for the expansion of understanding over time. This means that insights may be partial and subject to ongoing refinement.

Receiving a series of repeated "no" answers might also mean that the question itself is disharmonious, or that there is a problem in the way we are relating with the CC. Again, through a procedure of elimination it can be verified if, for example, the problem is a disharmonious question that exceeds appropriate limits. This may include questions that encroach upon another person's inner space. As will be discussed in Chapter Five, using our consciousness for healing purposes necessarily involves discovering the inner thoughts or attitudes of a person, which is not an encroachment because it is an integral aspect of restoring harmony within the person or situation. But questions that exceed this healing purpose, just to satisfy our curiosity about a person or issue, or a quest for knowledge about the cosmos, cannot be addressed. If this is the case, we may receive alerts to the presence of such disharmonies, for example through Hexagram 60 (Limitation): "*Unlimited possibilities are not suited to man ... To become strong, a man's life needs the limitations ordained by duty and voluntarily accepted.*" At this point, we need to simply withdraw focus on the other person or our own situation. The CC will also inform us when we are relating in a servile way or feeling mistrust towards the CC or our communication process with it. Sometimes the problem is simply impatience to understand a point, and we might be informed of the need to compose ourself before continuing, such as in Hexagram 32 (Duration): "*There are people who live in a state of perpetual hurry without ever attaining inner composure.*" Encountering such issues should not involve any type of judgment (such as, "I am doing it wrong"); this is simply part of discovering what comprises harmony and disharmony and the reasons for it. Through this process, we are also building a trusting relationship with the CC and getting to know how it relates with us and our constructed self.

A particularly challenging aspect of relying on asking "yes/no" questions is when we are not centered or when pursuing a misguided line of inquiry, despite receiving warning Hexagrams. This can lead to confusion and misinterpretations. It is quite easy to lose focus or get ambitiously caught up in our own assumptions, especially when engaging in a long session. This can be avoided by proceeding slowly, stopping regularly to again become centered, and if in doubt, asking the CC for guidance such as, "Am I in a harmonious place to continue with this inquiry?" It is important to not take it too far by becoming servile, such as asking this type of question frequently. The problem of servility is discussed later in this Chapter.

But if the ego persistently intrudes by ignoring warning Hexagrams, then asking dichotomous questions in an attempt to verify interpretations will undoubtedly lead to misinterpretations of the guidance. This is because the CC relates only with our true self. It protects its own integrity as well as ours by not engaging with the ego. This does not mean that we must be completely free of our constructed self in order to work with the CC. Certainly one of the major aspects of having a working relationship with the CC is to discover how the ego or constructed self is blocking our growth and harmony in life.

Unobstructed communication with the CC occurs when in a centered state, because then we are in touch with the true self and momentarily detached from the ego, even while we are exploring and identifying the false ideas and attitudes that characterize the constructed self. If during a session a disharmonious state of mind begins to intrude, the CC may provide warnings, such as in Hexagram 38 (Opposition): *"When opposition begins to manifest itself, a man must not try to bring about unity by force, for by doing so he would only achieve the contrary..."* or Hexagram 4 (Youthful

Folly): "*Without this modesty ... there is no guarantee that he has the necessary receptivity, which should express itself in respectful acceptance of the teacher. This is the reason why the teacher must wait to be sought out instead of offering himself. Only thus can the instruction take place at the right time and in the right way.*"

In my experience, the CC will always provide Hexagrams to our true self so that we are able to realize how the ego is intruding. Until this realization occurs, the CC cannot engage in answering yes/no questions that attempt to verify our interpretations of whatever issue is being discussed. If dichotomous questions are persisted, then we will find that we are communicating with the constructed self in these responses, and not the CC. Some warnings about the presence of this problem might be expressed in Hexagram 31 (Influence/Wooing), "*The influence produced by such mere tongue wagging must necessarily remain insignificant,*" or in Hexagram 52 (Keeping Still), "*serves a master stronger than himself.*"

This does not mean that the CC is turning away, withdrawing, punishing or retreating. It is not moving away from us. It is simply remaining in the background, waiting. It is always present and accessible, through the "kindliness of its nature," always willing to answer any sincere call for help. This is because the CC continues to flow through our true nature, even when disharmonious energies may block our access to it. We are reminded of this point in Hexagram 25 (Innocence/The Unexpected): "*We cannot lose what really belongs to us, even if we throw it away.*" This quote continues in its direct advice: "*Therefore we need have no anxiety. All that need concern us is that we should remain true to our own natures and not listen to others.*" The CC helps us to develop the clarity and strength to "remain true to our own natures," by retreating from ("not listening to") the incessant voices of the constructed self within us or other people.

Once it dawns on us how the ego might be intruding in the

session, then we can verify our insights about this through another Hexagram. At that point, we can see more clearly what the obstructing attitude was. It is also at this time that we may receive a Hexagram confirming we are back on the right track and can resume the session.

It has definitely *not* been my experience that the CC responds to ego intrusions during a session with "annoyance" or any form of judgment toward us, such as described in another section of Hexagram 4: "*If mistrustful or unintelligent questioning is kept up, it serves only to annoy the teacher. He does well to ignore it in silence, just as the oracle gives one answer only and refuses to be tempted by questions implying doubt.*" The CC does not use disharmonious methods such as intimidation or pressure in relating with us. Blind obedience, forced trust and obsequious approaches are also disharmonious because these attitudes damage our own integrity. And if feeling stuck in mistrust or doubt, we can always seek help to understand how to become free of these obstacles. Overcoming these types of obstructions in our relationship with the CC contains valuable learning experiences about protecting our integrity, which can then be transferred to our relationships with other people and the world.

Fixed Ideas About the I Ching

As described in Chapter One, some people misuse the *I Ching* as a form of entertainment or as an object to be studied, rather than as a methodology for discerning a Cosmic Perspective and a return to harmony. In preparation for writing this paragraph, I asked what the Cosmic Perspective is regarding such misuse and received the following phrases from Hexagram 34 (The Power of the Great): "*warning....there is danger that one may rely entirely on one's own power and forget to ask what is right....the oracle says that perseverance (i.e., perseverance in inner equilibrium, without excessive use of power) brings good fortune....One can give up a belligerent, stubborn way of acting and will not have to regret it."*

As also mentioned in Chapter One, some of the language in the *I Ching* portrays patriarchal and cultural references. If viewed as a sacred text, or if interpreted literally, then it will be impossible to discern the intended meanings of the Hexagrams. The point bears repeating: the CC uses the text in a relational process to communicate with the individual. This means that we need to approach interpreting the Hexagrams in a fluid and dynamic way that is entirely dependent on the unique situation being addressed. Chapter Two discussed some methods to bring ourselves into a calm state so that we can establish an energetic connection between our true self and the CC. With receptivity and perseverance, we soon learn how to interpret the unique guidance that the CC is offering.

Sometimes fixed doubts may obstruct the process of receiving guidance. These may include doubts about the authenticity of our relationship with the CC, uncertainty in our communication process with it, and hesitation in trusting our perceptions of the inner truth being shown about a given situation. It might not be immediately obvious when such doubts are invading our psyche. At times there may be a just a vague feeling of unease, which should prompt a person to investigate further. Or such doubts might manifest through feelings of resistance to what the CC is trying to show us during an *I Ching* session. Clues may be given about the presence of these obstructions in Hexagram 12 (Standstill): "... *it becomes impossible to make our influence count*," referring in this case to our being closed to the CC.

A large part of removing our conditioning involves developing the clarity and strength to consciously reject false ideas and attitudes that we have acquired. It requires strength because these elements of conditioning may be quite prevalent within society or our own inner circle of acquaintances, and this prevalence alone can exert pressure to conform, either consciously or subconsciously. So both clarity and strength are needed to keep our own counsel in the midst of the group. In order to do this, clarity must always come first because it provides the foundation for strength. If we are not clear on how or why something is disharmonious, we will vacillate in our commitment to reject the false pattern that has been dominating our thinking or influencing our behaviors.

Hexagram 45 (Gathering Together), speaks directly to this dilemma: "*The situation is this: people desire to gather around a leader to whom they look up. But they are in a large group, by which they allow themselves to be influenced, so that they waver in their decision. Thus they lack a firm center around which to gather. But if expression is given to this need, and if they call for help, one grasp of the hand from the leader is enough to turn away all distress. Therefore they must not allow themselves to be led astray. It is undoubtedly right that they should attach themselves to this leader.*" The "leader" refers to the CC, or the intelligent forces of harmony, whom we look to for guidance. It can also refer to the voice of our true self. Those who have experience in working with the *I Ching* are familiar with the sense of relief that is felt after receiving help to clearly see the ways in which we have allowed ourselves "to be influenced" by our training and by what other people say.

The CC does not test us in any way when we are trying to understand the meaning of its guidance in a Hexagram. As mentioned in Chapter Two, we might project or transfer problematic attitudes that we had in our relationship with parents onto our relational process with the CC. For example, this is evident when reacting defensively or feeling hurt upon discovering that we misunderstood some aspect of the guidance we had received. There might be an underlying fear of punishment for making mistakes. In these cases of defensiveness, we may receive feedback such as, "*Coming upon a sincere man, one fails to recognize him because of general estrangement*"

(Hexagram 38, Opposition) or *"He would like to ally himself with another but his good intentions are misunderstood"* (Hexagram 45, Gathering Together). But if we persevere in the learning process, and continue to clarify the intended meanings, we will discover that the CC helps us to identify the specific attitudes blocking our relating with it. Eventually these obstacles can be transformed into another important step in our growth process as our connection with the CC is re-established, as expressed in Hexagram 45: *"... this is the right course. For it may cause the other person to come to his senses, so the alliance sought and so painfully missed is achieved after all."*

Since it usually has taken many years to establish ingrained patterns of conditioning, it might require repeated guidance to gain clarity about the particular issue being deconstructed. There is no shame in returning again and again to the CC for help in regaining or deepening our clarity about the issue. With each new insight gained, we are expanding the strength needed to follow our own inner independence. However, the point is freedom, not the attainment of perfection, and the CC will help us become aware if such lofty goals are influencing us.

While the quest to understand something from a Cosmic Perspective is, in itself, a harmonious goal, sometimes the ego may intrude by seeking to know more than what is appropriate. Whether driven by curiosity, a quest for superiority over others, or fear that we need to know everything in order to be safe in life, such motives are disharmonious energies that block a relationship with the CC. Or we might start to ask questions on a tangential topic. The CC addresses such situations, for example, in these phrases from Hexagram 62 (Preponderance of the Small): *"If one overshoots the goal, one cannot hit it."* In our quest to understand something, our true self *"seeks an audience with his prince."* But if the ego tries to take advantage by exceeding limits, the relationship becomes blocked:

"*If not successful in this, he does not try to force anything*" because "*if one were to go on endeavoring to force his way to the goal, he would be endangered.*" Hexagram 25 (Innocence/The Unexpected) also describes this situation: "*If one acts thoughtlessly ... success will not be achieved. Innocent action brings misfortune.*" The "innocent action" is the attempt of our true self to comprehend something but when the ego takes over, it creates the "misfortune" of an obstruction in our relationship. To underscore the point, the CC may offer this further guidance from Hexagram 62: "*He who in times of extraordinary salience of small things does not know how to call a halt ... he deviates from the order of nature.*" The reference to the "extraordinary salience of small things" speaks to the blessing in attaining the Cosmic Perspective, which in this case, is one "small" piece of the Perspective. If we then try to grasp more than what is possible or appropriate for human beings to understand, we exceed natural limits and "deviate from the order of nature." The CC points to these natural limitations that apply to humans in Hexagram 10 (Treading/Conduct): "*Heaven and the lake show differences in elevation that inheres in the natures of the two.*" The "differences in elevation" is not referring to a hierarchy of superiority and inferiority, but to the "elevated" Perspective of the CC, of which human consciousness cannot fully grasp. This Hexagram continues with, "*Among mankind there is necessarily differences in elevation; it is impossible to bring about universal equality.*" Again, this is not referring to hierarchies within human society or in humans' relationship with the CC; instead, it speaks to the truth that there are some aspects of the Cosmic Perspective that are beyond human purview and comprehension. The CC reveals only that which aids us in the evolution of our consciousness.

Servility

Developing a partnership with the intelligent forces of harmony involves an interdependent relationship: we learn how to approach with sincerity and, over time, we realize that it approaches us in an authentic, respectful way. It supports our integrity and the development of our true self. It guides us in a direction that furthers our independence from reliance on any "authority," including people, institutions, or ideas. It also will help us become free of relating to the CC as an authority over us, including servile attitudes that diminish our autonomy; in this way, it helps us to trust our developing connection with our true self. Some clues telling us that servility is present might at times be quite direct, such as in Hexagram 4 (Youthful Folly): "*A weak, inexperienced man, struggling to rise, easily loses his own individuality when he slavishly imitates a strong personality of higher station.*" The references to hierarchical categories, along with the overt mention of slavish imitation, is a clear plea to respect ourselves in this alliance with the CC. This sentiment is similarly expressed in Hexagram 45 (Gathering Together), "*But of course there is also the possibility that people gather around him not because of a feeling of confidence but merely because of his influential position.*" Another clue that we have slipped into a servile approach is given when the CC underscores a line from Hexagram 54 (The Marrying Maiden): "*a situation not altogether compatible with self-esteem.*"

While our relationship with the CC involves a type of intrinsic reliance, this does not consist of a blind, subservient following of guidance, or forcing ourself to believe something without a thorough understanding of the points involved. The metaphorical "leader" mentioned frequently in the text includes the CC, but we are also simultaneously learning to follow the leadership of our true self as we expand our perceptions of the inner truth of a situation. Even sincere gratitude for help received can be taken too far if it becomes groveling. So it takes time to understand the difference between a true interdependent relationship with the CC, versus a servile, dependent one.

A challenging aspect of servility can develop when using the coins to ask yes/no questions. Certainly a degree of dichotomous questioning is necessary in order to clarify the specific guidance because there is a range of possible meanings in a given situation. Our understanding of the span of possibilities becomes more focused as we grow more familiar with the Cosmic Perspective. Gradually we learn which metaphors are inherently disharmonious, such as references to hierarchical and patriarchal relationships, for example. Once we have learned that a particular idea is true (harmonious) or false (disharmonious), it becomes easier to understand and intuit the intended guidance.

But overuse of asking yes/no questions can inhibit understanding. This happens when we begin a session proposing our interpretation of a situation before giving the CC the opportunity to guide us in a Hexagram. This contrasts with starting the session posing a question such as, "Is there a disharmony I need to investigate related to ____?" Then we proceed with Hexagrams if the answer is affirmative. It is easy to slide into a dependent relationship, however, when using the technique of asking yes/no questions. For example, we might need help to discern a plan of action. If we ask, "Is this action harmonious?," we might receive a no answer. To clarify, we need to ask, "Does no mean that this action would be disharmonious?" If the answer is again no, then we need some Hexagrams to reveal the issue. It could be that there is a problem with our approach, meaning that we are expecting it to tell us what to do rather than helping us become clear so that we can make our own decisions. Or it could mean that it wants to provide a larger picture for us, and for this we need a series of Hexagrams. A more helpful approach might be something like, "What is the Cosmic Perspective of taking this action?" and then being led through the necessary Hexagrams.

The constructed self has a vast repertoire of convoluted rationales and assumptions, which can create doubt and uncertainty that block the true simplicity of communication. We may even fall into suspicion that the CC is testing or punishing us in some way when caught up in confusion. At all times, the CC protects its own integrity, as well as the integrity of our true self, as described in Hexagram 41 (Decrease): "*Only where such delicacy of feeling exists can one give oneself unconditionally and without hesitation,*" and "*To render true service of lasting value to another, one must serve him without relinquishing oneself.*" The CC "serves" us through its unconditional help, and it does this within the context of maintaining the integrity of both parties. The CC will always attempt to inform our true self when any disharmonious attitude is interfering. Over time, we can recognize how the CC lovingly responds to ego insurgencies. It does not "throw itself away" on our ego when it is dominating: therefore, it cannot answer "yes/no" questions during this time when the ego mind is trying to pursue a point. Catering to the ego only makes it grows stronger, as any parent knows when a child is having a temper tantrum. It is a hugely important aspect of our own development to be able to recognize when ego attitudes are dominating, whether in ourself or others.

Misinterpretations

Some degree of misinterpretation is bound to occur as we encounter ingrained false ideas that are serving as the lens from which we view an issue. While the *I Ching* speaks of "danger" in such misunderstandings, these occurrences actually have great utility in the process of unlearning false ideas that obstruct our growth. Even a seemingly small or subtle misunderstanding of something the CC is trying to point out must be clarified, rather than simply overlooked. The true danger is if we give up on our learning process.

Sometimes there may even be a tendency to "over interpret"

a particular piece of guidance. This can occur when we apply the text in a literal way, or jump to the conclusion that the guidance is referring to some profound issue. Certainly we can receive counsel regarding profound issues, but we might forget that seemingly mundane or ostensibly minor issues are also the subject of needed guidance. This includes disharmonious attitudes or ideas that we regard as insignificant or harmless and thus have been ignored. Trust in the communication process is deepened as we realize that the CC is responding to our inner thoughts and attitudes — not as a presiding judge — but as a reliable friend helping us to return to harmony.

We may be given a variety of clues when getting off track or falling into a misinterpretation during an *I Ching* session. These are indicators that the conditioned mind, represented often as the "inferior man," has intercepted what the CC is trying to explain. This is when an ingrained false belief hijacks the meaning of a line from the *I Ching*, effectively overriding leadership from the true self during a session. Such warnings may include: "*someone other than the chosen leader interferes*" and "*authority is not being exercised by the proper leaders but has been usurped by others*" (Hexagram 7, The Army).

Sometimes the realization that we have misinterpreted something occurs during the session and other times it might not be recognized until later. The CC may repeat the same Hexagrams that were misinterpreted in the following day or week, giving us the opportunity to clarify the intended guidance. Even if we take an action or follow some path based upon misinterpreted guidance, we eventually will discover the error if we keep working with the CC. The error or misinterpretation is not the "fault" of the CC or the *I Ching* and it is not our "fault" — it is simply due to ingrained false ideas. Taking responsibility for errors means bringing them to light for a full understanding, and is a cause for celebration rather than shame. Each revelation contains an element of relief from previously unrecognized and unresolved traps within our consciousness, as expressed in Hexagram 42 (Increase), "*A time of blessing and enrichment has such powerful effects that even events ordinarily unfortunate must turn out to the advantage of those affected by them. These persons become free of error, and by acting in harmony with truth they gain ... inner authority.*" This is not to say that we need to court errors in order to learn, nor that the CC wants us to experience adversity. The point is that everything that happens to us can be an opportunity to glean the Cosmic Perspective of an issue. But ultimately, "verification" of an insight is a process that occurs slowly, over time, from the fruits of our applied learning.

Observing how we respond to mistakes provides an important window into the state of our self-esteem. For example, when we discover that we have misinterpreted something regarding the guidance received, unresolved childhood traumas might trigger a sense of humiliation, guilt, intense self-blame or anger at the CC. We might react as though we were being treated unfairly, particularly if raised in an authoritarian environment. Even though a nourishing relationship with the CC is not a parental one, we might project child/parent conflicts onto this relationship, causing great pain if our experiential lens is one of harsh discipline and punishment.

At some point in our working relationship with the CC, we might in fact receive Hexagrams that mention punishment. As with all guidance, it is important to verify how the CC is using a particular word or phrase. For example, if may be helpful to ask, "Are you referring to this sentence as something that is cosmically true?" Or, "Are you pointing to an inherently false idea?" We may discover that the CC is underscoring a phrase that mentions punishment in order to highlight false ideas that we have introjected or that are commonly accepted in society. Through this questioning, we realize that punishment, for example, is never part of the Cosmic teaching process.

Sometimes it may take a day or more to attain clarity. If caught in a cycle of confusion, it may be best to walk away for awhile and return when more composed. Then, when later reviewing the session notes, the message often emerges quite simply. After working with the CC around a difficult stumbling block to our understanding, we might receive acknowledgment of having successfully moved through it, such as in Hexagram 12 (Standstill), *"The time undergoes a change. The right man, able to restore order, has arrived,"* or in Hex 40 (Deliverance), *"The hindrance is passed, deliverance has come. One recuperates in peace and keeps still. This is the right thing to do in times when difficulties have been overcome."* To "recuperate in peace" includes not engaging in any self-blame or self-recriminations, in order to simply feel the sense of relief and gratitude for no longer being trapped in that particular obstacle, and being able to continue moving forward.

Obstinacy

While the constructed self is manifested in unique ways for each person, one characteristic seems to be common: the intransigent nature of the ego. Aside from outright destructive acts, this is one of the most dangerous aspects of the constructed self. It is easy to spot in others, less easy to identify in ourself, and quite difficult to eliminate. It can be seen in a stubborn refusal to change a behavior or attitude, even when we realize it is harmful to ourself, others or the environment. When challenged to question false assumptions and viewpoints, the constructed self might deploy various tactics to resist change, such as defensive rationalizations or harassing forms of self-talk and doubts about the feasibility of making needed adjustments. In these cases, the CC and our true self bear the brunt of such complaints: *"Naturally one is subjected to much criticism"* (Hexagram 53, Development/Gradual Progress).

Messages From the Body

Because the body operates as an energetic functional whole, we are gifted with an innate ability to detect the presence of disharmony directly through our physical states. It is an aspect of our inner warning system which, in my experience, operates mostly on an unconscious level. Paying attention to messages from the body, and investigating their meanings with the help of the CC, is one of the essential methods for bringing unconscious conflicts to the level of awareness so they can be addressed. Sometimes unconscious struggles may manifest in the form of subtle bodily reactions, such as fits of sneezing, coughing, gastrointestinal disturbances or headaches, for example. Other more serious bodily responses may result from long-term inner conflicts, false beliefs, or discordant attitudes. These problematic elements may form aggregated disharmonious energies that cluster within a major organ, such as heart, brain or lungs, or in a system of functioning, such as the circulatory or musculoskeletal systems. Ultimately these energetic disharmonies disrupt cellular functioning which may eventually result in the development of illness or disease.

Rather than blaming the body for the manifestation of these symptoms, a pathway to healing can be found by embracing and understanding the underlying message. In working through my own forms of obstinacy, I have experienced how disharmonious thoughts, feelings and behaviors represented energies that negatively affected my body in a multitude of ways. However, working with the CC to dissolve particular disharmonious energies relieved the various physical symptoms that were associated with these energies. This healing action can also weaken any aggregates or clusters of disharmonious energies that may be present within a particular organ or system, which will be discussed further in Chapter Five.

Breaking Free

The underlying drives or motives for obstinate attitudes and be-havior patterns can be understood and gradually dismantled through a working relationship with the CC. Sometimes it takes a shocking event, such as an accident or debilitating illness, to break an obsti-nate, self-defeating pattern. Even if such misfortune occurs, we can harvest gain from it if the experience becomes a turning point, as described in Hexagram 16 (Enthusiasm): *"A sober awakening from false enthusiasm is quite possible and very favorable."* Our growth process includes developing the clarity to recognize these ego patterns as *"the work of deceitful persons who have wormed their way in"* (Hexagram 53, Development/Gradual Progress), which are obstructing the development of new ways of being in the world.

There are several sections in the *I Ching* that directly address the intransigent ego, particularly in Hexagram 43 (Breakthrough/ Resoluteness): *"He would like to push forward under any circum-stances, but encounters insuperable obstacles....This is due to the obstinacy with which he seeks to enforce his will. If he would desist from this obstinacy, everything would go well. But this advice, like so much other good counsel, will be ignored. For obstinacy makes a man unable to hear."* This quote speaks to the challenging aspect of such stubbornness when working with the CC. Even when present-ed with the gift of a Cosmic Perspective or inner truth of a situation, we may reject it. This happens when the constructed self is firmly stuck in a particular viewpoint. Ultimately, the constructed self does not want to give up a disharmonious pattern because it feels entitled, self-righteous, resentful or any other variety of deluded rationales. This not only blocks the ability to listen to and embrace the guidance being given, but if carried on indefinitely, it obstructs the evolution of consciousness because it prevents learning.

A true test of our inner strength is seen in how we respond to obstinacy, both in ourself and others. If we are in the midst of an obdurate argument with the CC about an issue that we are trying to work through, it will continue to offer guidance in how to return to the true self. With practice, it is possible to develop the ability to walk away from the ego's insistent voices so that we can compose ourself and later resume our learning. This requires firm inner strength to set limits on our own ego, or entails withdrawing from arguing with another person's ego. Such strength is developed over time, as we learn hard lessons from experiencing the distressing effects that obstinacy has on our body, our relationships and overall well-being.

The CC does, however, speak about "forbearance" as an aspect of harmony when working to dismantle aspects of the constructed self. This is mentioned in Hexagram 18 (Work on What Has Been Spoiled/Decay) as *rectifying the mistakes of the past with forbearance.*" Learning to have forbearance toward our own and others' mistakes is a process that develops slowly and organically as we gain increasing clarity about the Cosmic Perspective. Forbearance is not forgiveness, but rather an attitude grounded in a clear understanding of the motives or causes within us that produce disharmony. Gaining clarity about what is harmonious is one of the main purposes of the "student-teacher" relationship with the CC. Under certain conditions, however, anyone could become vulnerable to slipping back into disharmony or entertaining false ideas. Even if total banishment of the ego were possible, it is not necessarily an appropriate goal to pursue if this entails making the constructed self a hated object, or elevating the struggle as an all-consuming and exhausting endeavor. Breaking free from conditioning is to allow disharmonies to dissolve, so that we may "cross the great water" or become in tune with the true, authentic self. From here, we experience tranquility in the small things, nourish others without seeking recognition, and find ourself continually renewed and supported until we reach the natural point of transition from the physical body of this lifetime.

CHAPTER FIVE

RESTORING HARMONY

Having mastered the ability to attain (or regain) a state of inner harmony means that a person has become capable of dissolving active elements of the constructed self when they arise. This can be thought of as the ultimate achievement in self-responsibility. It does not mean being completely, permanently, and always "free of ego." Rather, it means consistency in recognizing disharmonious elements if and when they emerge in one's own being, and dissolving them. Such consistency and reliability is described in Hexagram 10 (Conduct): *"He is true to himself and travels through life unassailed, on a level road."* This is no small feat. It represents the outer manifestation of the evolution of one's consciousness. It represents the ability to use one's consciousness to facilitate the gift of healing, or the restoration of harmony, within the self. When a person has become familiar with this way of being, then it becomes possible to initiate the dissolution of disharmonious elements that are present within other people or situations, for healing purposes.

As discussed in Chapter Two, human consciousness may be thought of fundamentally as an expression of energy. This energy is manifested through our physical body, thoughts, feelings, attitudes and actions. All people possess the freedom of choice as to how these energies are expressed. Self-governance means making conscious decisions about how we conduct ourself through all these forms of expression. This requires heightened awareness of the presence of our own energies and the ways they affect our total well-being, including relationships with others and the outer world in general. Heightened awareness of our energies includes the ability to utilize our innate capabilities for purposes of transformation.

In a session concerning the development of this Chapter, the CC pointed to the correct use of the *I Ching* as a way to facilitate transformation and healing. It first underscored the following phrases from Hexagram 50 (Ting/The Cauldron): "*the Book of Changes, fostering and nourishing of able men, pertaining to a refined civilization.*" The session continued with Hexagrams that addressed escaping the "dangers" encountered in our exposure to the many forms of disharmonious influences within human societies (the amalgamation of people's constructed selves), describing this as "*repetition of danger.*" In Hexagram 29 (The Abysmal/Water), the CC pointed to our living among fellow humans, and the various challenges this may entail, as "*an objective situation to which one must become accustomed.*" A group of people is described here as "*water that comes from above and is in motion on earth in streams and rivers.*" In this instance, "water in motion" refers to human beings living within societies ("in streams and rivers"). The dangerous aspect of our living situation is described in this same Hexagram: "*a ravine is used to symbolize danger; it is a situation in which a man is in the same pass as the water in a ravine.*" The reference to "the same pass as water in a ravine" describes our living in proximity to the constructed self of other people and the difficulties this may involve. The disharmonies created by other people often present obstructions great and small that must be dealt with in one way or another: "*If in difficult times we want to enlighten someone*" (Hexagram 29). The question is how. This same Hexagram offers a solution for overcoming this danger: "*The window is the place through which light enters the room.*" The remainder of this Chapter focuses on how the window of a person's consciousness may become opened and the ways in which the light of transformation may enter.

Using Power

From a Cosmic Perspective, much of human suffering is related to the disharmonious use of power. But it is possible to learn how to correctly or harmoniously use "power" through the effective use of our energy, although the methods for this usage are the exact opposite of how we usually conceive of using power. The *I Ching* describes some of the ways that energy moves within the forces of harmony: "*the power of the shadowy, the force of the small*" (Hexagram 9, The Taming Power of the Small), and "*gentle penetration*" (Hexagram 57, The Gentle/Penetrating, Wind). These describe how invisible energies operate both within and across the consciousness of human beings, as well as how influences from the CC penetrate to our consciousness. Such movements within the forces of harmony are described in Hexagram 61 (Inner Truth): "*The wind blows over the lake and stirs the surface of water. Thus visible effects of the invisible manifest themselves.*" Hexagram 9 discusses utilizing these subtle energies to create transformations, the basis of which is characterized as the absence of force: "*power actually lies with the weak.*" Weakness refers to innocuous, or harmoniously using the energy of consciousness to create change, rather than resorting to outer actions that are not informed by an awareness of the inner truth of a situation.

The reason these invisible energies are able to create transformations within ourselves and others is due to the presence of the true self within every human being, no matter how disharmonious the constructed self may be outwardly. The CC underscores this essential point in Hexagram 8 (Holding Together): "*Water flows to unite with water, because all parts of it are subject to the same laws. So too should human society hold together through a community of interests that allows each individual to feel himself a member of a whole.*" In the context of creating transformations, the metaphorical "community of interests" refers to recognizing the existence of the true self in human consciousness, which is reflective of the Cosmic Consciousness, thus making the individual a "member of a whole." The fact that some individuals may become completely cut off from access to their true self, speaks to their process of evolution rather than the non-existence of their true self. A metaphor for the presence of a person's true self that is being completely blocked by the constructed self is described in Hexagram 38 (Opposition): " ... *although they live in the same house they belong to different men; hence their wills are not the same but are divergently directed.*"

The harmonious use of indirect and "small" methods to create transformations may seem counterintuitive from the perspective of the constructed self, or from the ways societies usually approach the need for change, as in resorting to various forms of force that destroy the integrity and life force of human beings, other animals and our environment. Instead of relying upon external forces, we join forces with the Cosmic Consciousness by asking for help and then confidently rely upon it for harmonious interventions, thereby creating "*a truly modest union*" (Hexagram 11, Peace). If forceful methods are contemplated, guidance may point to warnings such as those from Hexagram 39 (Obstruction), "*the direct way is not the shortest,*" and Hexagram 26 (The Taming Power of the Great), "*where men are concerned, wild force should not be combated directly; instead, its roots should be eradicated.*"

Embracing Limits

Hexagram 60 (Limitation) offers guidance for living harmoniously when encountering disharmony. The quote below describes how we can avoid disharmony within ourself, and therefore within our life situations, by "voluntarily" accepting the natural limits that apply to human life on earth and living among human societies. All individuals possess the freedom to make decisions, and it is within the freedom of each moment that we exercise our choice for both inner and outer actions. In keeping with the theme of "water" as representing consciousness, the following quote from this Hexagram offers the image of a lake (a body of water with defined borders) as pertaining to the limits that apply to humans, while water itself (Cosmic Consciousness) is "inexhaustible" or unlimited:

"A lake is something limited. Water is inexhaustible. A lake can contain only a definite amount of the infinite quantity of water; this is its peculiarity. In human life too the individual achieves significance through discrimination and the setting of limits. Therefore what concerns us here is the problem of clearly defining these discriminations, which are, so to speak, the backbone of morality....To become strong, a man's life needs the limitations ordained by duty and voluntarily accepted. The individual attains significance as a free spirit only by surrounding himself with these limitations."

The previous Chapter discussed learning how to apply harmonious limits to ourselves for the purposes of our own well-being. This Chapter extends that discussion to address how to protect ourself from the disharmony of other people's constructed self, and to extending protection to someone else if it is indicated. One of the most important limitations to understand in effectively using our consciousness relates to correct purpose.

The CC makes clear that in order to successfully apply necessary limits on someone's disharmonious actions, we must first be willing to apply limits to ourselves. This point is directly addressed in Hexagram 60 (Limitation): *"Limitations are also indispensable in the regulation of world conditions....The limitation must be carried out in the right way if it is to be effective....If, however, a man in a leading position applies the limitation first to himself, demanding little from those associated with him, and with modest means manages to achieve something, good fortune is the result."* We take a "leading position" whenever we recognize a disharmonious situation that is affecting us. From a Cosmic Perspective, it is never appropriate to accept mistreatment or any situation that harms our integrity. This may include something seemingly mundane, such as an arrogant attitude displayed toward us, all the way to the extreme of physical harm.

Effective Self-limitation

In order to set limits effectively in an outer situation, it is absolutely necessary to first dissolve the disharmonious reactions that occur within ourself, so that we regain a state of inner harmony. The energetic forces of transformation cannot be transmitted through a disharmonious channel. Then, from a position of inner quiet and clarity, a person can apply the steps outlined later in this Chapter. Through relying on the help of the CC, we are using "modest means to achieve something," thereby creating "good fortune." The above reference in Hexagram 60 to "demanding little from those associated with him" means refraining from imposing forceful responses: these may include demanding an apology, pointing out the person's inappropriate behavior, holding inner resentments, or viewing the other person as inferior, hopeless or evil. And if our purpose in setting limits is infected by motives of superiority or self-righteously trying to "correct" someone, then these attitudes also need to be dismantled within ourself, with the help of the CC.

Dissolving our negative reactions is not only necessary for transformations to occur, but also for our own well-being because these disharmonious energies will eventually harm our total consciousness, namely, our body and psyche. Similarly, feeling hopeless, depressed, impatient, or aggravated about the need for setting limits with someone (e.g., "he should know better!") are also responses from our constructed self. These attitudes are discussed in Hexagram 47 (Oppression/Exhaustion): "*He who lets his spirit be broken by exhaustion certainly has no success,*" and "*At first he wants to push ahead, then he encounters obstructions that, it is true, mean oppression only when recklessly dealt with. He butts his head against a wall and in consequence feels himself oppressed by the wall.*" When caught up in angry reactions to someone's behavior, we will unavoidably be faced with more obstructions as a consequence, and thus "butt our head against the wall." Then, in addition to facing the problematic behavior of the other person, we have compounded the issue through our ego's intransigent reactions (head butting), which means we have "recklessly dealt with" the issue, causing further inner distress and failure to restore harmony in the situation. It can be very challenging to dismantle negative reactions to offensive behaviors, especially if conditioned to believe that such responses are expected, natural or justified (e.g., "of course you should be outraged!").

Again, the purpose of learning to apply a Cosmic Perspective to our way of life is not for the attainment of self-perfection. Nor does using our consciousness mean assuming responsibility for saving the world from suffering and destruction. The CC will provide warnings if such motives are present, such as exhibiting "*titanic aspirations that exceed one's power*" (Hexagram 1, The Creative). In learning how to harmoniously respond to these types of challenging situations, we are actively engaged in furthering the evolution of our consciousness. Through this development, we are becoming capable of using our consciousness to help create more peaceful, transformative relationships with other people and situations that are within our sphere of influence.

The Art of Protection

In my experience, the fundamental basis for self-protection centers on preventing the constructed self from interfering with the natural state of harmony, whether within ourselves or in relationships with others. As previous Chapters have addressed, mastering the ability to manage and limit our constructed self allows us to connect with our true nature. When we have, so to speak, become "trustworthy" in this process, then we can be of use in facilitating the transformation of situations. Trustworthiness encompasses reliability in self-limitation, as well as consistency in receptivity to guidance from the CC. As Hexagram 31 (Influence/Wooing) points out, *"It is true that if we cannot be influenced ourselves, we cannot influence the outside world."*

Within the rubric of restoring harmony, there seems to me to be two different situations with respect to facilitating transformation. One situation is for the purpose of protecting our own integrity from encroachment by setting limits on someone's disharmonious actions. Despite the fact that a person's constructed self is dominating in a situation, the hidden true self can be accessed within this transformational process, as alluded to in Hexagram 7 (The Army) in the metaphor of, *"Ground water is invisibly present within the earth."*

The other situation is for the purpose of protecting or healing someone within our sphere who is in need — but only when led to do so. Under the guidance of the CC, this type of influence has the profound function of allowing the "light of transformation" to enter the consciousness of others, as described in Hexagram 30 (The Clinging, Fire): " ... *the function of light with respect to time.... The great man continues the work of nature in the human world. Through the clarity of his nature he causes the light to spread farther and farther and to penetrate the nature of man ever more deeply."* Here the "great man" refers to the CC, which "penetrates" the consciousness of humans, in this case, through the interdependent participation of the person making a request for transformation or healing. A similar idea is expressed in Hexagram 39 (Obstruction): *"Here we see a man who is called to help in an emergency.... because he is really called to the task, the power of his spirit is strong enough to attract helpers whom he can effectively organize, so that through the well-directed co-operation of all participants the obstruction is overcome.*"

Effortless Action

As we learn to become reliable in restoring harmony within ourself, our usefulness may be applied more widely. Such benefits are directly mentioned in Hexagram 41 (Decrease): "*It is unselfish and good when a man, after completing his own urgent tasks, uses his strength in the service of others, and without bragging or making much of it, helps quickly where help is needed.*" The reference to one's "own urgent tasks" refers to dissolving the influences from our constructed self. This allows for the gradual development of increased clarity and inner strength which can be utilized in situations to facilitate transformation.

Facilitating healing must be done within correct parameters. Guidelines are offered in Hexagram 4 (Youthful Folly), "*The only thing that furthers is to prevent transgressions*" and in Hexagram 49 (Revolution/Molting), "*We must be satisfied with the attainable. If we should go too far and try to achieve too much, it would lead to unrest and misfortune. For the object of a great revolution is the attainment of clarified, secure conditions ensuring a general stabilization on the basis of what is possible at the moment.*" Making requests for limits to be set are only for the two purposes mentioned: the protection of our own, or someone else's integrity, within a defined situation. It is not for the purposes of punishment, satisfying a goal designed by our ego or to create a change that is beyond our scope. The reference to "ensuring a general stabilization" means restoring harmony within the confines of the situation. Understanding the inner truth about a particular situation, and the appropriate limits that need to be applied, can only be accomplished when we are open to guidance, as described in Hexagram 55 (Abundance): "*The ruler is modest and therefore open to the counsel of able men.*" In this instance, the "ruler" refers to the true self, which is "modest" or receptive to guidance from "able men" or the CC.

If we engage in heroic or "titanic aspirations" by trying to influence situations that are outside of our purview, then we risk creating obstructions in ourself. This can happen when observing distress that someone else is experiencing. It is important, however, to not make assumptions about the situation based on surface appearances. The only way to ascertain the inner truth of the situation is to consult with the CC. In many cases that involved healing for others, I have been made aware of their need for help through a dream. The exact nature of the help needed was then verified and explored through consultation with the CC using the *I Ching*.

This does not mean that every dream about a person is a call for help, nor that witnessing the struggles other people encounter in their path of learning is an indication that we should attempt to intervene. If witnessing another's distress is triggering a desire to help, or if in doubt about appropriate action, then it is important to find the inner truth, or Cosmic Perspective, of the situation so that we do not misuse our compassion.

Attaining the Cosmic Perspective is an important form of self-healing because any inner conflict, anger, depression or angst we might feel in observing another's distress is no longer contributing to disharmonious energies that may already surround the other person or situation in question. In these instances, it can be helpful to simply request that the active elements of their constructed self be dispersed, so that they can temporarily gain access to their true self. But again, this is successfully done when in a state of inner harmony, after having dissolved any disturbing reactions within ourself.

There may be times when help is needed immediately and there is no time or opportunity to consult the CC about the inner truth of the situation. We may frequently find that our simple and spontaneous actions, without thinking, are exactly suited to the needs in such situations. But there may be some instances where action is not possible or appropriate. Here again, if skilled in attaining a calm inner state, then it is possible to simply take a moment to gain composure and then ask the CC to disperse the other person's constructed self.

Therefore the key to effortless action, paradoxically, requires an initial effort directed at managing our own inner state. This means, as described in the beginning of this Chapter, setting limits on dissolving our own disharmonious responses before transformational healing can be accomplished. Our responsibility in this type of partnership with the CC is described in Hexagram 2 (The Receptive): "*When anyone is called upon to work in a prominent but not independent position, true success depends on the utmost discretion.*" The reference to "discretion" underscores the importance of our being free from any ego interferences. Once a state of clarity and inner harmony has been reached, we can proceed with the limit-setting request and then simply let go of any further effort, allowing the forces of harmony to respond naturally, as "*The wind blows over the lake....Thus visible effects of the invisible manifest themselves.*"

Strategic Self-restraint

With simple daily practice, governing our own inner state becomes second nature, which makes calling upon help for healing interventions a smooth and easy process. But without this practice and experience, falling into disharmonious reactions to another person's obstinacy or harmful behavior inevitably creates obstructions in ourself and in our relationship with the other person. The energies inherent in such reactions block the transformational process.

The *I Ching* frequently mentions the need for caution and restraint in such situations; this is done by inwardly and outwardly "retreating" from any critical or harsh response, thereby allowing harmonious interventions to be enacted. Hexagram 10 (Treading/Conduct) advises how to avoid compounding the problem when faced with disharmonious behavior: "*In terms of a human situation, one is handling wild, intractable people. In such a case one's purpose will be achieved if one behaves with decorum. Pleasant manners succeed even with irritable people.*" Applying this guidance may entail a simple disengagement from disagreeable discussions with the other person, or dropping the matter completely. Contrary to popular belief, such a retreat does not mean that we are "giving in" to the other person's demands or viewpoint. Instead, we are protecting our own integrity or, as Hexagram 12 (Standstill/Stagnation) describes it, "*Success in a higher sense can be ours, because we know how to safeguard the value of our personalities.*" To "safeguard the value of our personalities" means protecting ourself from the frustration, helplessness or fury that undoubtedly accompanies a head-on engagement with someone's stubbornness. Becoming entangled with an obstinate person or obdurate situation can occur either outwardly, in what we say or do, or just as problematically, inwardly through what we think and feel about the person or issue. But if we can manage to regain inner composure, then an effective request can be made for limits to be set. Applying this type of strategic self-control results in a much more constructive use of our energy, which is expressed in Hexagram 60 (Limitation): "*.... energy that would otherwise be consumed in a vain struggle with the object, is applied wholly to the benefit of the matter in hand, and success is assured.*"

Relying upon the forces of harmony achieves justice without involving any outward actions on our part, and without further reinforcing obstinate reactions in the other person by trying to make them see the light of reason. Hexagram 36 (Darkening of the Light) speaks to just such a situation: "*One should not needlessly awaken overwhelming enmity by inconsiderate behavior. In such times one ought not to fall in with the practices of others; neither should one drag them censoriously into the light.*" Even though we may be "in the right" about an issue, we still must protect the integrity of the other person's true self. Otherwise we would "fall in with the practices of others" by fruitlessly trying to use disharmonious methods to restore a state of harmony. This theme is also addressed in Hexagram 6 (Conflict): "*To carry on the conflict to the bitter end has evil effects even when one is in the right, because the enmity is then perpetuated. It is important to see the great man, that is, an impartial man whose authority is great enough to terminate the conflict amicably or assure a just decision.*" This same Hexagram advises us to rely upon the CC to create a resolution: " ... *an arbiter in a conflict who is powerful and just, and strong enough to lend weight to the right side. A dispute can be turned over to him with confidence.*" Once we have successfully dissolved any negative reactions to the situation, we are in a position to re-establish a connection with our true self and can proceed with a request for transformation. It is from this place of inner harmony that "*repeated and well-founded complaints should not fail of a hearing*" (Hexagram 49, Revolution).

Steps in Facilitating Healing

To transform a disharmonious situation requires our true self to create an energetic connection with the CC. As described throughout this Chapter, establishing this connection means that we first dissolve any disharmonious elements within our own consciousness, including any doubts about the existence of the other person's true self, before making a request for an intervention. Doing this allows the CC to penetrate the consciousness of the other person, in response to our request for help in restoring harmony in situations where someone is overstepping boundaries. When the ego is thus encroaching, the *I Ching* often refers to it as a "dangerous" situation. Hexagram 29 (The Abysmal/Water) describes the type of assistance that is available when "*there is the honest intention of mutual help in danger*" — assistance is "*Simply handed in through the window.*"

We don't need to try to specify what the resolution should look like because the forces of unanimity inherently restore whatever elements need adjustments in the best way possible. These transformations occur outside the conscious awareness of the recipients. It does not result in any negative or painful responses in the person. It does not involve any type of "crisis of healing," such as when a high fever might break an infection. I never speak to the person about the healing request. For both the recipient and the person requesting transformation, it is a natural gift of life that is free of recognition, obligation or credit. And for the person facilitating the healing, it is a gift full of wonder and gratitude.

Contrary to popular myths and historical traditions, facilitating healing in this way does not require special qualifications, training, or endorsements from others. Participating in such transformations is a potential gift that lies within the nature of the ordinary person who is experienced in accessing the true self. And making such access is not magical: it simply takes awareness and determined practice. So once you have ascertained that it is appropriate to facilitate healing in the situation, meaning that it is within your domain of action, then you can proceed with the steps outlined below.

Six Steps

There are six general steps to follow in the process of facilitating healing. The **first step** is accessing your true self. This essential step is done simply by taking a few moments to quiet the mind and body to attain a state of inner calm. This may take some practice, but it does not require learning any special meditation techniques. From this calm and centered state, the **second step** is to rely on the guidance of the CC to investigate the underlying inner truth of the specific situation affecting the person in need. This might also include identifying any disharmonious feelings or ideas you have regarding the person or situation, because the presence of such elements within yourself could block healing. Depending on the nature or complexity of the problem, completing this step may take awhile in order to gain a full understanding of the situation so that you can proceed in the process. The **third step** involves identifying which specific disharmonious beliefs, attitudes or intentions need to be dissolved within the consciousness of the person in need. Again depending on the nature of the situation, this dissolution may involve just a single disharmonious belief, feeling or intention, or a series of them. Your exploration of the inner truth of the situation in the previous step provides the context for your being able to ascertain the specific disharmonious elements to be dissolved. The **fourth step** is to ensure that you are in a harmonious state, and if so, proceed with a request that the CC which flows through the other person dissolve each of the disharmonious elements that have been identified. This step is made possible by the energetic connection between your true self and CC. The **fifth step** is to inquire if there are any aggregate disharmonious energies in the recipient that could interfere with the energy of healing. This involves identifying the *number* of aggregates and their general *location* in the body, such as a major organ (heart, brain, lungs, etc.) or a system of functioning, such as circulatory, gastrointestinal, or musculoskeletal. In my experience, roughly about a third of all healing requests included the presence of these aggregates. In these cases, you simply include a request for their dissolution. This allows for a weakening of the aggregated disharmonious energies within their body. The **sixth and final step** is to let go of the situation in its entirety. This means not worrying about whether healing is occurring, how long it might take or any state of mind where you are giving the situation your attention. This would only interfere with the energy of healing.

It is important to ascertain each day from the CC if you have effectively completed your part in the transformation, or if you need to repeat step four which consisted of making a request for dissolution (and step five, if aggregates are involved). Sometimes healing only requires a single request. Other situations may require you to repeat the request for dissolution once daily for two or more days. But if by the third day, you are informed that it still needs repeating, then you need to find out if there are any subtle disharmonious feelings within yourself that are blocking the healing. If this is the case, you simply use the same process to identify the nature of the disharmony, and dissolve it within yourself. Often, this only needs to be done one time in order for the original healing request to be unblocked, or completed. However, if you cannot imagine that the true self in the other person even exists, because of the nature or extremity of the person's disharmonious behavior, then you need to stop and re-examine your attitude with the guidance of the CC. The number of times a request for healing needs to be repeated is not necessarily related to the apparent simplicity or complexity of the situation.

Confidence and trust in this healing process can only come through repeated experiences. Even seemingly mundane situations can be addressed in this way, and these become part of the process of gaining trust in this new way of approaching life. In my experiences over the years, dozens upon dozens of problematic situations have been successfully resolved using these steps. By "successful," I mean that a problem was remedied without my taking any outer action, and usually without the involvement of external sources of help that societies often depend solely upon, such as doctors, lawyers and protection agencies. Restoring harmony can be applied to situations as simple as stopping a dog's incessant barking in the middle of the night or a neighbor's raucously loud domestic dispute, to more serious problems such as someone's successful recovery from drug addiction or avoidance of deportation in a court hearing.

In another example, I made a healing request for a friend who was experiencing deeply embedded emotional and behavioral disharmonies. I became aware of her need after I investigated a disturbing dream about her. In the dream, I found her lying face down in a swimming pool, nearly drowned. I pulled out her heavy, unconscious body from the edge of the pool and, after yelling for help, I began compressions on her back to release the water. I investigated the dream and after about three pages of notes from relevant Hexagrams, identified disharmonious elements involved between her and her partner. I made the first request for dissolution of these elements, but due to various other activities, I actually forgot about checking on the status of it until three days later. I was informed that I needed to repeat the request, which I did. Early the next morning, I experienced this dream: I was visiting my friend in her new house. She led me inside and I began to wander around to look at the place. I went into the kitchen. Despite the fact that this was a "new house," I had somehow seen the previous kitchen. I was amazed to see how the room had been beautifully remodeled. It was gleaming everywhere: the entire space was freshly painted white, with white countertops and all white appliances. She had removed one of the walls, so that natural light filled the space.

The CC confirmed that the dream signified her healing. But I needed to continue requesting dissolution of disharmonious elements within her partner for another two days, because I discovered lingering resentments I felt toward him which needed to be cleared before his healing could be completed. Sometime later, I learned that a long-term physical illness my friend had been experiencing was much improved, and conflicts with her partner were disappearing.

Response to Violence[4]

A scenario that most people eventually face in life is how to respond when harmed by someone or by a threatening situation. The decisive question is how to respond in a way that elicits the helping energies of the Cosmos, and does not perpetuate cycles of suffering and violence. For those who have experienced the murder of a loved one, it is the ultimate shock in life.

Many years ago, three of my colleagues were killed in a mass shooting event. The person who shot them later killed himself. There were many witnesses to these murders, who later recounted the cruel words he spoke to my colleagues before killing them. Following the murders, I had been working with an organization that was helping some of the family members of people who had been killed, which included attending support group meetings. Each week, I saw the intense suffering of those trying to come to terms with violent deaths of family members. One week after the homicides, a woman I did not know (whom I will call Susan) came to a meeting. She was extremely angry and sobbing as she explained how she was consumed by frightening thoughts and visions about the time of her friend's death, the cruel words spoken by the man with the gun, and the terror of the moment. Psychologists term this type of reaction "re-enactment fantasies" and flashbacks, causing great suffering as loved ones compulsively imagine the murder scene as a waking nightmare. The grief counselor at this session told Susan that even though she did not know her, she "loved her." I could see that Susan was immediately rejecting this comment and it was not the type of "help" she needed. After others in the group had spoken, I offered Susan my understanding of the murder event: to us, it appears the person suffers, but in reality, a protective mechanism takes over whereby the shock of the event causes a separation of the body from the mind and senses. Everything happens in slow

---

[4] *Excerpt from Letters to the Human Race, MC Flenniken, 2016.*

motion as the person intellectually takes in what is happening ("he's going to shoot me"), but there is no emotional reaction to it. What appears to us as a terrifying scene may not necessarily be what the person involved actually experienced. Susan cried bitterly, saying she wished she could believe that, and then stormed out of the meeting. The grief counselor was not too happy with me because in her perspective, painful feelings needed to be experienced and validated. In other words, her ideas of healing meant experiencing the full gamut of suffering or a catharsis, and she felt my comments suppressed Susan's expressions of pain.

Later that evening, I inquired with the CC if my comments to Susan had been correct, and received a strong "yes." I was then advised to ask for help in assisting Susan to see her friend's death from a Cosmic Perspective, and to request a limit to the re-enactment images she was having. I did this once daily; after three days, I was informed to stop because the situation was resolved.

By the end of that week, I received a call from Susan. She sounded very excited and happy, and I was curious about her response. She explained that the morning after the support group meeting, a woman at her workplace, who had survived an armed robbery, described exactly the same process I had mentioned about the separation of mind and body during a shocking event. Susan said, "When two people tell me the same thing in 24 hours, I listen!" She had not experienced a single re-enactment image that entire week. While she still was grieving, an enormous burden had been lifted and she no longer suffered from terrifying images. Several weeks later, I spoke with Susan and she was continuing to do well, with no further flashbacks.

Susan's healing and her ability to see the situation from a new perspective was not from her simply receiving new information alone. The hidden, helping aspects of the Cosmos are always available when we sincerely seek to understand something from a Cosmic Perspective. The idea that healing requires a cathartic release of painful emotions is simply untrue. This does not mean, obviously, to repress feelings. It means that when a situation is understood from a Cosmic Perspective, and a request is made for help in letting go of false notions and their attendant emotions, then healing and solace are natural consequences. Relief from the pain of grief does not indicate an absence of love. When the true meaning of each unique situation is understood, then something new is learned about the nature of the Cosmos and our place in it, bringing profound gratitude and peace.

In seeking help from the CC to understand the death of my colleagues, the point was emphasized that while they had gone through a transformation, their lives had not ended. Therefore, in using the term "death," I am referring strictly to the end of life in a physical body, but not the end of consciousness. It also emphasized that understanding their deaths from a Cosmic Perspective was not possible as long as my viewpoint was fixed upon ideas about "monsters," "heroes," "justice" and "tragedy," as was the prevalent refrain within the community in response to this shocking event. My experiences showed me that as long as I was willing to suspend fixed beliefs, and sincerely seek help to understand the Cosmic Perspective as much as I could at the moment, I was always helped.

Blessings of a Simple Warning[5]

In this next experience, I had an unexpected opportunity to discover in a very direct way the true meaning of this quote from Hexagram 43 (Break-Through/Resoluteness): "*If an individual is careful and keeps his wits about him, he need not become excited or alarmed. If he is watchful at all times, even before danger is present, he is armed when danger approaches and need not be afraid. The superior man is on his guard against what is not yet*

---

[5] *Excerpt from Letters to the Human Race, MC Flenniken, 2016.*

in sight and on the alert for what is not yet within hearing; therefore he dwells in the midst of difficulties as though they did not exist. If a man develops his character, people submit to him of their own accord."

One day during an *I Ching* session, I was directed to line 3 from Hexagram 62 (Preponderance of the Small): "*If one is not extremely careful, somebody may come up from behind and strike him. Misfortune....At certain times extraordinary caution is absolutely necessary....There are dangers lurking for which they are unprepared. Yet such danger is not unavoidable, one can escape it if he understands that the time demands that he pay especial attention to small and insignificant things.*"

In my past experiences when having received this passage, I have interpreted this line metaphorically, warning me about a disharmonious energy that I needed to investigate, such as negative thoughts generated from within me or someone else that were having harmful effects. In this particular session, however, I discovered that the prior interpretations did not apply. So I identified the meaning of the line through a simple series of dichotomous questions. I am not sure it would have occurred to me to pose the right questions, or even been open to the possibility of actual physical violence, if not for the murder of my colleagues several years earlier.

The answers pointed to a cherished friend, living in the other side of the country from me, and who was in potential physical danger. Further questioning revealed that someone who was unknown to my friend, in a workplace environment, intended to bring harm through violent action. I knew to not ask any further detailed questions, such as the type of violence or the time frame involved, as this would only heighten my anxiety and interfere with healing. I was then led to call upon the energies of the CC to negate this person's violent intentions, which I completed per the steps described above. After a brief meditation, I asked if my request had

been made appropriately. No, it had not. Further questioning revealed that fear was interfering. I calmed myself and centered again.
Finally, upon the third attempt of calming myself and repeating the
healing request, I was informed that it had been done effectively.

I remember feeling nervous for my friend after this session, but
resisted the urge to call her to check if everything was alright. I had
learned by then to trust the transformational process, so I was able
to turn the matter over to the Cosmos and let it go at that time. The
next day I was informed, to my astonishment, that the request had
been taken care of and no further action was necessary. It seemed
surprising to me that such a serious matter was taken care of so
easily, with only a single limit-setting request. I had considered the
question: Would I ever know that my friend was truly safe from this
potential assailant? However, my prior experiences and confidence
in the trustworthiness of relying upon the Cosmic Consciousness
prevented this type of fear and wondering from taking hold. I knew
that if I was meant to receive any external verification, it would
come at the right time, on its own, which enabled me to let go of
worry and further questioning. Because of the confidence I had
built from accumulated experiences in relying upon the CC, I truly
believed that the issue had been taken care of and gave it no further
attention. Letting go of watching for results is a crucial aspect of
working with Cosmic energies.

Days and weeks passed, and still my friend was fine. One
Sunday morning, approximately ten months later, one of my family
members announced she was going out to buy a newspaper. Pur-
chasing a hard copy newspaper had become a rare event in our
home. Later in the afternoon, my eye glanced over the newspaper
sections strewn across the coffee table. I saw a front page headline
announcing the arrest of a man in the town where my friend had
worked. I read that the local police had been notified because of
threatening emails a coworker had received, prompting a search of

the man's apartment. An arsenal of 25 rifles and other guns, as well as several thousand rounds of ammunition, were found in the apartment along with other emails he had sent threatening to kill coworkers. As those who reside within the USA realize, such stockpiling of weapons and ammunition is unfortunately all too common. But the man's arrest was described as a great shock to neighbors because, as they reported, he seemed "so quiet and gentle."

There are many aspects of this experience that felt extraordinary: being forewarned about the violence, the ease and simplicity in which the violence was averted, the way I received "notice" of resolution from the newspaper article, and how I was able to let go of fearful watching for my friend's safety. A simple warning, given quietly to a single person, a hidden blessing reverberating unbeknownst to its recipients; this is the way that the forces of harmony function, when we are open to it. It seems extraordinary because we are so accustomed to mindsets that denigrate this truth. But if we are open, we can always be helped in seeking to comprehend the Cosmic Perspective of a situation, to see beneath surface appearances. Cosmic protection is not a right, but is an accessible blessing.

By doing my part in completing the cycle of harmony in situations, my relationship with the CC is further developed and shaped. I do not submit myself to a higher being; I submit to learning what harmony means in a given situation. I no longer try hard to trust, but strive to recognize fears that erode trust. Instead of berating myself for once again falling into conditioned beliefs and attitudes, I lay down the whip of perfection. I embrace the CC that flows through me, and with this, the constructed walls of misperception crumble, creating tiny openings for the forces of harmony to seep through.

www.ingramcontent.com/pod-product-compliance
Lightning Source LLC
Chambersburg PA
CBHW011239120626
46549CB00009B/3333